3 2044 128 578 119

D1570808

An Awkward Embrace:
The United States and
China in the 21st Century

An Awkward Embrace:
The United States and
China in the 21st Century

Dan Blumenthal and Phillip Swagel

The AEI Press

Publisher for the American Enterprise Institute

WASHINGTON, D.C.

Distributed by arrangement with the Rowman & Littlefield Publishing Group, 4501 Forbes Boulevard, Suite 200, Lanham, Maryland 20706. To order, call toll free 1-800-462-6420 or 1-717-794-3800. For all other inquiries, please contact AEI Press, 1150 Seventeenth Street, N.W., Washington, D.C. 20036, or call 1-800-862-5801.

Library of Congress Cataloging-in-Publication Data

Blumenthal, Dan.
  An awkward embrace : the United States and China in the 21st century / Dan Blumenthal and Phillip Swagel.
      p. ; cm.
  Includes bibliographical references and index.
  ISBN 978-0-8447-7235-6 (cloth)—ISBN 0-8447-7235-6 (cloth)
  ISBN 978-0-8447-7236-3 (pbk.)—ISBN 0-8447-7236-4 (pbk.)
  ISBN 978-0-8447-7237-0 (ebook)—ISBN 0-8447-7237-2 (ebook)
  1. United States--Foreign relations—China. 2. China—Foreign relations—United States. 3. United States--Foreign relations—21st century. 4. China—Foreign relations—21st century. I. Swagel, Phillip. II. Title.

E183.8.C5B55 2012
327.7305109'05—dc23

                                2012021297

Printed in the United States of America

Contents

Acknowledgments

We would like to thank all of those who played such a large role in making this book possible. First and foremost, we are grateful to Christopher DeMuth and Arthur Brooks, former and current presidents of AEI, for providing us with the opportunity and encouragement to take on a project such as this. We would like to thank the Smith Richardson Foundation for its generous financial support and patience as this project came to fruition and Danielle Pletka and Lauren Kimaid of AEI for their assistance and guidance.

We also owe much to our honorable interviewees on several research trips to China and in meetings in the United States. Insights from these discussions inform the content of this book. A special thanks goes as well to Nicholas Eberstadt for many discussions over the years on China's future, the importance of demographic factors, and the utility of having national security experts consider economic viewpoints and vice versa.

We would like to thank our publishers at AEI and Goldberg McDuffie for their work to publicize the book. Finally, several talented research assistants and interns were invaluable in conducting research and putting the final product together. We are especially grateful to Michael Mazza and also recognize the dedicated work of Laura Coniff, Leslie Forgach, Lara Crouch, Grace Warrick, and Aaron Cantrell.

Introduction

Dan Blumenthal and Phillip Swagel

China's growing global power is one of the most hotly debated topics in U.S. foreign policy. China's rapid economic growth and important roles as trade partner and primary lender to the United States have made the future of the U.S.-China relationship a key economic issue. At the same time, China's economic development has been matched by an increasingly capable military and an assertive posture in Asia. Given its size and dynamism, it is not surprising that China would once again have a central role in the international economic and political systems after more than a century of diminished standing. That time is now at hand, and the impact of China on the United States and the global order has become central to the strategic debate.

In the simplest terms, debate about China's role in the world is dominated by two broad schools of thought, most comfortably (if not entirely accurately) labeled the "Good China" school and the "Bad China" school. The former is informed by an economic- and business-driven view of China as a "rational actor," the latter by a national security assessment of the so-called China problem. In general, the Good China school embraces an optimistic future, and generally sees the relationship as dominated by trade and financial ties that are beneficial for both nations. The continued deepening of these ties will provide an incentive to China to play a constructive role in global affairs, both economic and strategic. The Bad China school increasingly worries about a future in which Chinese growth translates into assertive and problematic behavior.

Students of the "Good China" school have tended to dominate U.S. foreign policy toward China. Indeed, policies to contend with China as a strategic competitor have enjoyed little sustained support among the American political elite. Richard Nixon attempted to enmesh China in the international system; as he declared:

> We simply cannot afford to leave China forever outside the family of nations, there to nurture its fantasies, cherish its hates, and threaten its neighbors. There is no place on this small planet for a billion of its potentially most able people to live in angry isolation.[1]

Every U.S. president since Nixon has essentially followed his approach to China. The primary goal of this approach is to ensure that China has substantial incentives—namely, economic benefits that accrue to China through its linkages to the United States and other nations—to undertake responsible and cooperative policies. A secondary, if less explicit, goal is to "tame" China or socialize it to accept the Western-made international system. From this perspective, China policy is a win-win proposition in the sense that both China and the United States benefit from the economic relationship.

A serious case can be made for the success of this policy. Since Deng Xiaoping inaugurated the economic revolution in 1979, China's involvement with international trade and its embrace of an economic system that is increasingly (though far from entirely) market-based has unleashed the talents and energies of the Chinese people and lifted hundreds of millions of Chinese out of poverty. For China, the benefits of its integration into the world system have been remarkable, as China has telescoped the economic growth that many countries took a century to achieve into a few remarkable decades. As a consequence, influential voices advocate for even more integration into existing global political and economic structures, for China's development into a responsible great power, and even for greater political liberalization as a means by which to foster continued economic growth.[2]

Many argue that China's economic growth will in fact lead to broad liberalization, both economic and political. China's rise is therefore seen as a net good, even if the process of political liberalization unfolds slowly. Indeed, it is hard to argue with the fact that the United States and China trade to the overall benefit of both countries.[3] Continued Chinese growth will mean the availability of low-cost consumer and business goods and services for U.S. families and businesses and a growing market for American goods and services within China. Capital flows from China help keep U.S. interest rates low and thereby support higher household spending and business investment than would otherwise be the case. These capital flows likewise help to finance the U.S. government's yawning fiscal deficit. China has also made limited progress in some dimensions on political liberalization: overly noisome dissenters still look out from behind bars, and the Internet remains screened by the so-called Great Firewall, but Chinese society is far more open and pluralistic than it was three decades ago.

A final cornerstone of the Good China view of the U.S.-China relationship is the belief that governments act to maximize the welfare of their citizens and therefore ultimately reject policies that could lead to economic distention. Following this logic, conflict between the United States and China is a remote possibility: both sides have too much to lose.

International relations, however, are not restricted to the question of advancing prosperity. If history tells us anything, it is that neither individuals nor nations are purely economic creatures. Just as China has grown richer, more economically integrated, and more powerful, forces within China have risen that advocate against a wholesale acceptance of the international system.[4] Indeed, much of the Chinese political elite rejects political liberalization and is dedicated to the continued grip of the Chinese Community Party (CCP).[5] A Communist Party that sustains its monopoly on power, intent upon obtaining a dominant position in Asia, will, in all likelihood, lead a nation that emerges as a geopolitical rival to the United States.

For adherents of the Bad China school, the nation's soaring growth is not necessarily a net positive, as Chinese economic growth translates into prospects of acting on ambitions for increased military and political power. A particular strain of Chinese nationalism, reinforced by economic success, stokes grievances about past mistreatment at the hands of the United States, Japan, and Europe. China's strategic elites also seem to hold deeply rooted historic memories of Chinese regional hegemony.[6]

The combination of growing power and a growing, aggrieved nationalism is driving many within China's leadership to reject key aspects of an
American-led international system.[7]

When it comes to economic policy, China does participate in aspects
of the system that it finds useful, including trade agreements and multilateral institutions such as the International Monetary Fund, while fail-
ing to abide by strictures that might hinder near-term growth such as
respect for intellectual property. But the pushback on the United States
is much more notable on the security side, where the Chinese military
has consistently worked to develop military capabilities designed to
overcome U.S. military dominance. As China has become stronger, its
interests and ambitions have increased. This development need not pose
a threat to Washington. But the opaque manner and the character of
China's military buildup threaten to destabilize the international system.
Although currently the Chinese military acts mostly coercively (against
Taiwan, Vietnam, the Philippines, and Japan), its growing capabilities
may portend higher future levels of violence and outright aggression.

A China working to upend the American-dominated post–World War
II system will be a U.S. rival and a threat to U.S. allies in the Asia-Pacific.
China hawks are persuaded that opaque authoritarian governments
unconstrained by genuine political debates about allocation of resources
act to maximize their national power and prestige rather than merely
economic growth. This is the situation in China, where the lack of broad
political participation and the limited concern of the ruling party for the
population means policy is focused on the mix of military and economic
advances necessary to stay in power.

The central task for the United States, then, is to protect its interests
in the region by limiting China's ability to dominate Asia. This entails
increasing the U.S. security presence in the Asia-Pacific region and ensuring that no U.S. ally could be coerced by China. Should the rise of China
seriously erode American leadership, the United States will face a new
and complicated foreign policy challenge in the form of a global rival
with whom it is deeply economically intertwined. The United States is
accustomed to identifying countries as friends or foes. But China is both.
Should China continue to emerge as a great power that sees itself as
Washington's rival—and that acts as a rival—the United States will need to

practice a sophisticated statecraft that allows it to continue to benefit from trade and financial ties while at the same time limiting China's expansionism or countering the negative impacts of problematic Chinese behavior.

Crafting such a policy requires a clear understanding about developments within China itself. While all agree that China has grown tremendously over the past few decades and that much of the world, including the United States, has benefited from Chinese growth, it is also the case that China faces an array of demographic and social problems with which it must contend. These issues include an aging population, a decrepit social safety net, rising middle-class expectations, pervasive corruption, and rapid urbanization and environmental degradation that pose challenges for the quality of life today and will require the devotion of substantial resources in the future. On top of this, the legacy of China's one child policy will be a long-lived shift in the nature of Chinese society, as shrinking family networks—no siblings means no cousins—provide a smaller contribution to social stability.

Under conditions of dizzying economic growth, China has been able to build its instruments of national power while at the same time coping with these manifold social challenges; dramatic societal changes are more manageable when people are getting richer. But at some point in the near future, perhaps the very near future, China will face more difficult choices.[8] When choices must be made between social development and military power, will China indeed engage in "peaceful development" as some in Beijing insist is China's priority? Will it become a responsible great power, embracing what many call the "liberal international order," in order to focus on internal economic, political, and social development? Or will China instead pursue, even if gradually and incrementally, a project to restore itself to great power status in the face of social stresses (or perhaps to offset them)? If this latter course is taken, China might well seek slowly to bend the international rules to better accommodate its aim of dominating much of Asia.

The choices are not mutually exclusive. With continued economic growth, China can choose both to pursue its great power ambitions and to address social fissures at home. Problems will come, however, if growth falters, and choices must be made. In the wake of a serious economic downturn, China's leaders could externalize domestic pressures and rally the nation around foreign threats, imagined and real, as is common among authoritarians. Conversely, a turn toward a confrontational foreign policy could lead to diminished economic growth as other nations balk at continued economic and financial ties with a China that behaves in a threatening manner. The Chinese blockade on exports of rare-earth minerals to Japan in September 2010, for example, awoke other nations to the need to develop alternative sources for these essential items. This might be economically inefficient in a world of unfettered trade, but it is a rational policy to take out insurance against disruptive Chinese behavior. What is most difficult to know is whether further economic growth will spur such disruptive actions or instead prevent them by increasing the value to China of cooperation in the global economic system.

The debate about China's future often reflects more about the prognosticator than about the Asian giant. Economists, business leaders, and many professional China watchers reject the notion that those in Beijing who rescued the nation from Mao would imperil the vast material gains achieved over the past three decades. For security hawks, it is precisely that pride in China's great strides forward that could unleash dangerous nationalism and greater ambitions.

This book looks to reconcile these views, and to foster understanding about how modern China can nurture differing forces that hold great promise for a prosperous future while also portending immense danger to the United States and the existing global economic and security structure. Understanding China requires exploring forces of economic growth as well as nationalism and considering the relative power of different constituencies within the Chinese system. For U.S. policymakers, the imperative is to take steps that help achieve the benign and mutually beneficial future even as we gird against the worst.

Notes

1. Richard Nixon, "Asia after Viet Nam," *Foreign Affairs* 46, no. 1 (1967): 111–25.

2. C. Fred Bergsten, Charles Freeman, Nicholas R. Lardy, and Derek J. Mitchell, "China Debates Its Future," in *China's Rise: Challenges and Opportunities* (Washington, D.C.: Peterson Institute for International Economics and Center for Strategic and International Studies, 2009), 33–56.

3. Sino-U.S. trade has mushroomed over the last three decades. From 1987 to 2007, the value of U.S. exports to China grew from $3.5 billion to $62.9 billion; imports from China increased from $6.3 billion to an astounding $321.4 billion. See U.S. Census Bureau, *Foreign Trade Statistics*, http://www.census.gov/foreign-trade/balance/c5700.html (accessed November 2, 2010).

4. See Aaron Friedberg's analysis of the Chinese view on America's strategy and its impact on the U.S.-China security competition. Aaron Friedberg, *A Contest for Supremacy: China, America, and the Struggle for Mastery in Asia* (New York: W. W. Norton & Company, 2011), 120–41. See also Wang Hui and Rebecca E. Karl, "Contemporary Chinese Thought and the Question of Modernity," *Social Text* 55 (Summer 1998): 9–44. This article argues that contemporary Chinese cultural and social problems are linked to the values transmitted by the modern Western capitalist system, which have drastically altered the Chinese socioeconomic landscape in the last thirty years.

5. Bergsten et al., "Democracy with Chinese Characteristics? Political Reform and the Future of the Chinese Communist Party" in *China's Rise*, 58–60. See also Andrew J. Nathan, "China's Political Trajectory: What Are the Chinese Saying?," in *China's Changing Political Landscape: Prospects for Democracy*, ed. Cheng Li (Washington, D.C.: Brookings Institution Press, 2008), 25–43.

6. Gerald Chan, *Chinese Perspectives on International Relations: A Framework for Analysis* (New York: St. Martin's Press, 1999), 56.

7. Russell Ong, *China's Security Interests in the 21st Century* (New York: Routledge, 2007), 34–45.

8. China's growth is already slowing. If China's growth rate falls from the 9–10 percent per annum it had previously enjoyed for decades down to 5–6 percent, as some economists predict, it will be far more difficult to absorb the roughly 24 million people joining the labor force every year. This could call into question a key element of the CCP's continued rule: the successful migration of some 12 to 14 million poor rural farmers every year to the modern industrial and manufacturing urban sector. See Nouriel Roubini, "Hard Landing in China?" *Forbes*, November 6, 2008, http://www.forbes.com/2008/11/05/china-recession-roubini-oped-cx_nr_1106roubini.html.

1

China's Rise to Rivalry

Dan Blumenthal

The massive and rapid shift in the distribution of global wealth and power toward Asia is comparable in scale, and potentially in historical significance, to the "rise of the West"—the emergence of Europe as the world's leader in wealth and military power—or the rise of the United States to global preponderance that began in the nineteenth century. To a greater degree than ever before, America's future security and prosperity depend on what happens in Asia. If China decides to disrupt or attempt to upend the post–World War II Asian political system, the promise of the great transformation in the Asia-Pacific to foster international prosperity could go unfulfilled.

As Asia grows in prominence, it is worth restating America's key and enduring strategic objectives in the region. First, the United States should work to prevent the domination of Asia by a hostile power or coalition. Second, Washington should help shape an Asia that is "prosperous, peaceful and free."[1]

Why China's Rise Matters: U.S. Interests in the Asia-Pacific[2]

The minimal aim of U.S. strategy must remain what it has been for the past century: to preclude the domination of Asia by any single power or coalition of hostile powers. This is necessary to prevent others from threatening our security and prosperity through any attempts to control the region's resources, form exclusive economic blocs, or deny our physical

8

access to and through Asia. No one should doubt that the United States is and will remain an Asia-Pacific power, not only because of its geography, but also by virtue of its historic ties, past sacrifices, and enduring economic and strategic interests.

Preventing the domination of Asia by a hostile power also offers the best chance for the survival and continued spread of liberal democratic political and economic institutions and values—an expansion of liberty that has been underway in the region since the end of World War II and accelerated markedly in the past quarter century. The United States must continue to work with its friends and allies to preserve their security and to maintain a balance of power that discourages any possibility of aggression or coercion against them. By cooperating with the United States and with one another, democracies such as Japan, South Korea, Australia, and Taiwan can continue to focus the bulk of their energies on economic growth rather than dissipating resources on security competitions or even the pursuit of weapons of mass destruction. Continued peace and stability, even in the face of rapid shifts in the regional distribution of power, will also allow Asia's younger democracies time to consolidate their institutions of governance while enabling continued economic growth. A stable security environment could also help to dampen the spread of virulent nationalism, perhaps easing the way for liberal reform in countries such as China that have not yet made the transition away from authoritarianism.

It is very much in America's interest that Asia's future not look like its past—a past that was characterized by frequent conflict for much of the twentieth century, the domination of outside powers for much of the nineteenth century, and the hegemony of a single Asian state for much of its previous history. In the aftermath of the Cold War, U.S. policymakers set themselves the goal of helping to build a Europe "whole and free." Our long-range goal in Asia should be much the same. Working in conjunction with the nations of the region, we must help to build an Asia that is prosperous, peaceful, and free.

While not a perfect analogy, the history of the West is instructive. It was only when the nations of Europe converged on a common set of liberal democratic values and institutions that they were able to resolve their historic animosities, settle outstanding disputes, build trust, and eliminate barriers to the free movement of people, capital, goods, and ideas. After centuries of brutal conflict, war among the democratic nations that today comprise the European Union (EU) is virtually unthinkable. As recent events have shown, however, peaceful relations between Europe's democracies and its authoritarian neighbors, such as Russia, remain at risk.[3]

While an Asia prosperous, peaceful, and free would differ from Europe in many respects, these basic ingredients are as necessary for a successful Asia as they have been for a successful Europe. A prosperous, peaceful, and free Asia would be one that is not divided by militarized spheres of influence or along ideological lines or split into exclusive economic blocs. It would be a region shaped by free trade and economic exchange rather than by security competition. A prosperous, peaceful, and free Asia that respects the democratic process would not require the reintegration of every territory sundered by historical conflict because it would permit the peoples at the center of these disputes to determine how best to resolve outstanding differences. Festering territorial disputes must be resolved peacefully with a strong emphasis on self-determination, thereby gradually removing them as potential flashpoints for global conflict.[4]

Given Asia's transformation, and America's strong interest in the shape of that transformation, the character of China's rise is of utmost importance. China could become a responsible great power and help shape a prosperous, peaceful, and free Asia. Or it could become a more intense rival to the United States and shape a region characterized by security competition, disrupted or balkanized processes of trade and economic integration, and deep suspicion.

The U.S. role in shaping Asia's future is critical. No other country, coalition of powers, or set of institutions can underwrite Asia's security or provide the leadership necessary for the creation of liberal economic and political institutions. For the foreseeable future, America's foreign policy aims in the region must be backed by U.S. military primacy, aided by capable allies. Challenges to America's position are challenges to its vision of an Asia compatible with its interests.

The future of Asia depends greatly on whether China intensifies its security rivalry in order to change the Asian political system to suit its narrow nationalistic interests or whether it instead accepts the "Western" system dominating Asia today.

What Is a Rival in the Twenty-First Century?
What Is a Responsible Great Power?

The idea of great power rivalry seems antiquated in the twenty-first century. It is the condition that best describes relations between England and Germany in the latter part of the nineteenth century until World War I, Japan and the United States until World War II, and the Soviet Union and the United States throughout most of the twentieth century. In the former two cases, the countries were both friends and foes, deeply involved in bilateral trade, cooperating on some geopolitical matters, but also competing for prestige, power, and military dominance.[5]

Rivals are not enemies. They do not seek to conquer or to destroy each other, but they also will not hesitate to use force to protect their interests. Rivals have different, usually conflicting, views of how to secure their national interests. In Asia, the United States has implicitly outlined a path toward security, peace, and prosperity based on U.S. military dominance, strong alliances, trade liberalization, and the continued creation and strengthening of democratic institutions. The Asia-Pacific order that the United States favors also seeks to prevent exclusive economic or military spheres of influence. If Beijing has a different view of the regional order that best secures China and has the power to shape that order, the two countries will be rivals.

Successive U.S. presidential administrations have hoped to avoid such an outcome and have invited China to join the "family of nations," offering it a seat at the table as a responsible great power. The premise behind this approach is that the international system is dominated by groups of "responsible" states that behave in certain ways at home and abroad and work together to maintain a liberal political order. It has been American policy to encourage China to join this system since the presidency of Richard Nixon.[6]

The most sophisticated recent articulation of the idea that China is welcome into the international system as a "responsible power" came during the George W. Bush administration. In 2007, in remarks at the Peterson Institute, then-deputy secretary of state Robert Zoellick urged China to become a "responsible stakeholder," a country that works "with other major countries to sustain and strengthen the international systems that keep the world more secure, enable it to be more prosperous, and open opportunities for our peoples."[7] In another speech on this topic given in 2005, Zoellick argued that responsible stakeholders allow international law and custom to govern their external behavior.[8] They also work to strengthen the international system. Zoellick not only welcomed China into the "family of nations" but also asked it to play a greater role in strengthening international economic, security, and diplomatic affairs.[9] In his speech, Zoellick reaffirmed that U.S. policy has not been to contain China and weaken it.[10] Rather, U.S. policy is to strengthen China and welcome its rise.[11]

Zoellick's speech mirrored the arguments of scholars optimistic about the prospects of a peacefully integrated China into the Western-made international system. For example, Princeton scholar John Ikenberry argues that China "faces a Western-centered system that is open, integrated, and rules based."[12] The United States created this type of system after World War II to be universal and bring market economies closer together, while inviting others, who will play by the rules, into the system. Ikenberry states:

> [T]he U.S.-led order is distinctive in that it has been more liberal than imperial. ...Its rules and institutions are rooted in and thus reinforced by the evolving global forces of democracy and capitalism.[13]

Zoellick has also argued that the liberal international system has benefited many countries besides the United States, including China.[14] Given that, China should embrace the existing international system in all its aspects, and the system in turn will embrace China and provide a secure environment in which it can continue to develop and raise the standard of living for its people. Indeed, many with this view suppose that China has no choice but to join the liberal international system because that system is so strong that it can resist any country's attempts to change it.

This raises the natural question: if the Western order has already invited China's participation, and China is already benefiting from the system, then why do senior policymakers and scholars feel the need to explain the system to China and encourage it to become "more responsible"? Clearly,

China has not yet embraced the liberal order. Indeed, one worrisome possibility is that China will ultimately reject the role of stakeholder in the current international system and instead work to develop an entirely new one in which it is an outsider to the international security system and does not display greater respect for democracy, human rights, and existing international economic norms.

Zoellick pointed to several critical areas in which China's behavior does not contribute positively to the international system. Some of China's natural resource acquisition policy is mercantilist; its clumsy attempts to secure sources of commodities such as oil and gas impose higher costs on other nations without succeeding in the ostensible objective of safeguarding Chinese growth.[15] China's military buildup has been destabilizing.[16] China has done little to bring Iran and North Korea into compliance with nonproliferation obligations. China's attitude toward what it calls "splittism," by which it means efforts by certain geographically concentrated ethic groups such as the Uighurs to win greater autonomy or outright independence, is at odds with the liberal system's notion of how to deal with territorial or ethnic disputes.

Zoellick also identified perhaps the key source of anxiety about China's rise. He noted that the international order is largely dominated by democracies and free-market economies.[17] Democracies tend to believe that authoritarian great powers, which are abusive of citizens' rights at home, will likewise be more aggressive and less respectful of the rights of other countries and more secretive about their intentions. For these reasons, successive U.S. presidents have expressed the desire for democratic change in China. The Clinton administration spoke about "peaceful evolution," a process, it was hoped, by which a China increasingly open to trade and investment would gradually and peacefully evolve into a democracy.[18] Without explicitly saying so, all U.S. political leaders realize that China cannot truly be a responsible great power and close friend of the United States until it respects the rights of its people at home.[19]

Since the triumph of the "liberal system" that ended the Cold War, the United States and Western countries have argued about how best to preserve the system and spread its benefits. The Clinton administration, for example, declared that its purpose in foreign policy was to "enlarge" the community of democratic nations—in other words, to expand the liberal order.[20] It went so far as to use military force on mostly humanitarian grounds, without the approval of the United Nations, to stop ethnic cleansing in Kosovo, thereby demonstrating that the great powers would at times forcefully intervene in the affairs of other countries. The Bush administration was likewise adamant about its desire for democratic change within autocratic nations as the path to preserving the liberal order.

Both administrations welcomed China into an international order that the United States saw as useful for dealing with a new century's threats and opportunities. In the 1990s, Western countries intervened in several European countries without the sanction of the United Nations. From the Balkans to Iraq to Sudan, Western countries concluded that direct intervention in the affairs of sovereign nations was justified when those nations' regimes abused their citizens. As a result, the way the West defines what it means to be a responsible great power changed as well. The liberal order now demands that countries abide by international rules of economic and political behavior abroad and at home.

While the liberal order benefits and inspires many, some of its dimensions are profoundly offensive and even threatening to the CCP. China's party leaders question why it is anyone's business how it acquires critical natural resources. Why should any country have a say in how China treats what it believes are people within its own country—in Tibet, in Xinjiang? Why should anyone interfere in the matter of Taiwan, a territory China views as its own? Every rising power developed a powerful military; why should China be any different? China has its own problems to contend with; why should it help with other countries' problems such as those of North Korea or Iran?

Though China embraces parts of the international system, notably the trading system, it already rejects an international system that concerns itself with other countries' human rights records or expects too much of China. China will use its power to have its say about what can and should be of concern to great powers, and it will defend itself against any perceived encroachment on its internal affairs.

If China grows more powerful and rejects other parts of the international order that it finds threatening, it will not merely sulk in a corner and complain about Western-imposed international rules. China is likely to work against them instead and thus to work against U.S. interests. Because of its sheer size, economic and technological dynamism, and military capability, China is the one country that can rival the United States for power, prestige, and influence in the world.

An important caveat is in order. Great power competition between China and the United States is not inevitable. Rising powers and established powers do not always conflict. Take the example of the United Kingdom and an emerging United States. The United States and Britain were not destined to be allies. To the contrary, for much of the nineteenth century they were rivals. But as American power grew, leaders within Britain debated whether a rising America was a threat or merely a rival. Britain concluded that the United States was not a threat but in fact a potential ally, and over time, the two countries forged a "special relationship." There are many reasons why Anglo-American relations became friendly. For example, Britain concluded that Germany was a bigger threat, and powerful domestic constituencies argued that as Anglo democracies the two had a shared identity. Likewise, there are many reasons why Britain and Germany became rivals and eventually enemies, including strategic clashes, internal perceptions, and the push and pull of interest groups in each country.[21]

There is nothing preordained about America's relationship with China. Today, relations are characterized by a mix of economic interdependence and cooperation on the one hand, and suspicion and rivalry on the other. And the two powers are at peace. A key variable—perhaps *the* key variable—that will define Sino-American relations is how politics within the People's Republic of China (PRC) unfolds. Should the Chinese political system liberalize, other nations will undoubtedly become less suspicious of Chinese intentions.

Why China Behaves as a Strategic Rival: The Domestic Sources of Rival Behavior

As the United States continues to encourage China to behave responsibly, the way China thinks about its role in the world is changing. Though still authoritarian, Beijing is much more open than it was during Mao's rule. Moreover, it is no longer dedicated to a communist-versus-capitalist ideological struggle with the West. Rather, China has become a more traditional authoritarian power, albeit one with strategic memories and traditions of its own. Deng Xiaoping's opening of China to international trade and investment has resulted in a more pluralistic society. Minxin Pei has accurately described the contemporary Chinese system:

> The core features of a Leninist regime, such as the dominance of a party-state, the control by the ruling Communist party of the most critical economic and information assets, and the unhesitant use of the repressive power of the state to quash any organized challenges to its authority, remain largely intact. Yet, the Chinese Leninist party-state today co-exists alongside a very dynamic and liberalizing society.... In other words, Chinese politics today is authoritarian, but Chinese society is becoming more pluralistic, autonomous, and open.[22]

Because elite Chinese politics is still a relatively black box, it is difficult to identify the preferences of particular leaders. Analysts cannot readily point to one group of leaders and call them "hawks" or others "doves." It is equally difficult to point to groups of leaders who are economic liberals or economic populists. Moreover, competing preferences, perceptions, and worldviews may reside within the mind of a single leader. For example, it now appears that former Chinese president Jiang Zemin was both an economic reformer and a staunch hawk. Under his rule, China made enormous changes as it joined the World Trade Organization, but he also oversaw the largest military buildup in the post–Cold War era. He apparently wanted his legacy to include the return to China of all "lost territory": Hong Kong, Macao, and Taiwan. When confronted with military options against Taiwan in 1999 that he did not like, he ordered his generals to speed up China's military modernization.

Though analysts cannot easily identify hawks or doves or nationalists or liberals among the ruling clique, it is possible to identify more generic sources and pressures that shape Chinese foreign policy, and it is possible to make inferences about policy preferences based upon observations of Chinese behavior. Apart from the primary Chinese need for economic growth, which is addressed in a later chapter, there are three domestic sources that seem to dominate Chinese foreign policy, all of which push China to behave as a strategic rival.

The first is an aggrieved nationalism, at once a tool used to legitimate the CCP and an intensely held sentiment of many Chinese people. Both the CCP and the Chinese people feel a deep-seated need to regain China's former glory and to make up for lost time. The basic story is this: After its "century of humiliation," which lasted from the mid-nineteenth to the mid-twentieth century and in which the West and Japan preyed upon and destroyed its great civilization, China has finally gained the economic and diplomatic footing necessary to assert itself. Therefore, China must employ its newfound economic prowess and political clout to obtain what it increasingly calls its "core interests." The character of this kind of nationalism—themes of pride interlinked with an acute sense of victimization—causes China to interpret its disagreements with the United States and other Western nations as affronts to its interests that are intended to put China in its place.[23]

The second is a deep sense within the CCP that it is beleaguered and living in a hostile world. After the shock of Tiananmen and the collapse of the Soviet Union, the CCP felt that it was living on borrowed time. Like the Soviet Union, China is governed by a one-party Leninist dictatorship, which lords over a multiethnic and multinational empire. Watching the Soviet empire dissolve, as states such as Estonia, Lithuania, and Ukraine gained their independence, was a shock to the CCP. The CCP is thus highly sensitive to domestic protests and demonstrations that can threaten its monopoly on power and hold on its empire. Moreover, the CCP suspects that the real intention of the West and international institutions is to change the regime through containment and pressure, just as they pressured the Soviet Union into collapse.

The third domestic source is what might be termed a strategic culture of "realism." For our purposes, realism means a worldview in which nation-states must maximize their power to achieve security in an anarchic world. This worldview privileges the military instrument of statecraft: the use of force is effective in achieving political aims. The realist worldview is also highly suspicious of liberal notions of international politics, such as humanitarian interventions, peace through trade interdependence, human rights diplomacy, or democracy promotion. It is this worldview that most resists a role as a responsible stakeholder in an international system that all powers must uphold.

In addition to these three most important domestic sources of foreign policy, there are new influences on foreign policy found outside the CCP leadership. Today, CCP leaders must take into account, at least to some degree, domestic interests and voices outside the party-state as they conduct their foreign policy. CCP leaders must be attentive to increasingly prominent voices both within and outside the CCP, including those of the leadership of the People's Liberation Army (PLA), public intellectuals, authors, businessmen, and dissidents.[24] However, it appears that these voices are overwhelmed by those in power who seek to maintain the CCP's monopoly over politics and China's expansion as the dominant Asian power.

Nationalism. Chinese nationalism would not by itself lead the PRC to be a rival of the United States. Americans are proud of their country and can also be nationalistic. But the dominant form of American nationalism is linked with a sense of higher purpose, the upholding and promotion of certain ideals of political and economic liberty that are attractive to many others in the world. This type of nationalism links the United States to other countries with shared values and worldviews.

The nationalism of concern in the PRC is different. It has at its core a sense of grievance against the United States and some of its allies and irredentist claims on territory. Historically, Chinese elites defined China as the "[Central] Kingdom, the hub around which others revolve…a China destined by its superior culture to tutor (and in some degree, to control) others…"[25] The Chinese emperor had the "Mandate of Heaven" to rule all others. China had a universal and superior culture that influenced tributary states along its periphery. States now known as Korea, Vietnam, Indonesia, Burma, and to some extent Japan had to accept a lower place than China on the status hierarchy. For these states to conduct foreign relations with China, they had to accept a deferential role and pay tribute to the Chinese emperor. The natural order of the Chinese world was a status hierarchy with the Middle Kingdom on top.

The ravaging of China by "Western barbarians," beginning with the British Opium War of 1842, was thus a deep shock to Chinese leaders.

For Chinese leaders at the time, these countries had "technological superiority [that] gave them a power that neither their culture nor their methods of governance warranted."[26]

The shock of the Western destruction of the Chinese world order is still a deeply ingrained wound. Chinese schoolchildren still learn about the humiliations visited upon China by supposedly inferior Western cultures. The lessons include the imposition of extraterritorial legal rights for Western traders and unequal trade treaties. In addition, former tributary states were taken over by Western imperialists with their own universalistic pretensions. Indonesia was taken by the Dutch, Vietnam by the French, and Burma by the British. The Chinese world order traumatically collapsed. Even more humiliating was the loss to Japan, a country clearly thought to be lower in the Asian hierarchy, during the Sino-Japanese war of 1895. The Qing dynasty lost territory it nominally controlled, including Taiwan.

The century of humiliation, that finally ended with the victory over the Japanese in 1945, is still a powerful collective memory in China that conditions both elite and public attitudes toward China's external relations. Moreover, many Chinese believe the United States is at fault for the continuance of Taiwan's "separation" from China after the Japanese defeat in World War II.[27]

The fires of China's past humiliation can easily be fueled. In 1989, the CCP suffered the dual shock of countrywide demonstrations for democracy culminating in the massacre at Tiananmen and the collapse of former Leninist states in Eastern Europe and the Soviet Union. It was not difficult for a shocked and frightened Chinese leadership to reinvigorate a sense of aggrieved nationalism among the public. In the CCP's telling, the Tiananmen protesters were "conspirators" working with "hostile foreign forces" to make China weak again.[28] After Tiananmen, the CCP launched a "patriotic education campaign" playing to the public sense of grievance.

Children were taught that the United States and the West had brought down the Soviet Union only to make it weak. Calls for more political liberty or democracy from the outside were portrayed as ruses to weaken the PRC, akin to the ravaging of China by the West and Japan during the century of humiliation. The PRC was to grow strong through economic development and military prowess so that never again would "barbarians" or internal plotters conspire to weaken and humiliate China. The CCP would recover lost territory and restore Chinese greatness. This nationalist program required the retaking of Hong Kong from the British, of Macao from the Portuguese, and of Taiwan, now protected by the Americans.

In addition, any calls for more autonomy in parts of the old Chinese empire, which in some cases the PRC had re-conquered, were to be quashed. CCP elites have conflated holding on to the empire and regaining Taiwan with restoring the greatness or the "oneness" of China. While the CCP pushed this kind of nationalism on the Chinese people to sustain its continued monopoly on power, it was pushing on an open door: nationalism is deeply felt among large segments of the Chinese public.

The power of the century of humiliation narrative can be seen in both elite and popular reaction to the return of Hong Kong, for example. A popular 1997 movie, *Red River Valley*, told a tale of the Chinese, once victims, righting the wrongs of the past and thus victims no more.[29] The official countdown to the return of Hong Kong was called a countdown to the end of "national humiliation." When talks with the British became difficult, Chinese writers took great pleasure in portraying British governor-general Chris Patten as a blathering idiot.[30] Deng Xiaoping was lionized when he said publicly that China would decide how and when Hong Kong would return.[31] Some authors even brought up Margaret Thatcher's fall at the Great Hall of the People after a meeting with Deng Xiaoping in 1982. Although she slipped accidentally, Chinese commentators used the incident to show that Britain should be subordinate to China as it retook Hong Kong.[32]

With the British out of the picture, the United States is now seen as China's chief antagonist. In popular books and articles, the United States is portrayed variably as an arrogant, imperialist hegemon or a child whose history is so short it needs to be taught how to behave by the adult Chinese.[33] Around the time of the 1996 Strait crisis, Chinese media published photographs of Korean War veterans in order to stoke feelings of pride and confidence in Chinese readers, reminding them that in the 1950s the Chinese PLA defeated the most powerful military on earth in Korea.[4] When the United States dispatched two carriers to the Strait in response to Chinese aggressive shows of force against Taiwan in 1996, popular CCP nationalists like Chai Zemin, former ambassador to the United States, and Li Peng again invoked the "victory" over the United States in Korea as a warning to the Americans.[35]

The source of popular fury at the United States during the mistaken bombing of the Chinese embassy in Belgrade in 1999 was the widely held view that the United States had assaulted China's national dignity. The Chinese public did serious damage to the American embassy in Beijing; given that the area around the embassy is off limits to ordinary Chinese, this action was only possible with the concurrence of the local authorities. Some Chinese called for a national movement to seek personal donations to build aircraft carriers to stand up to the Americans.[36] Some accused their leadership of weak responses to American arrogance. Many Chinese believe the Americans bombed the embassy to keep China down.[37] The CCP, which had to balance other goals such as stabilizing the Sino-American relationship in order to keep the economy growing, called for students to return to school, and workers to go back to work. A similar dynamic was at work after a Chinese fighter jet collided with a U.S. EP-3 surveillance plane flying over international waters in 2001. Chinese behavior, including the holding of the crew, the righteous demands for an apology, and the taking apart of the aircraft, has a variety of explanations, but the CCP's need to respond to another national outrage was surely among them.

Such views are common in the wider Chinese public, and the view of Sino-American relations as dominated by conflict rather than common interest appears to be gaining currency among influential Chinese. The United States is hell bent, in this view, on maintaining its hegemony at China's expense and must be resisted.[38] Thus, there is reason for concern that the CCP is competing with segments of the Chinese population for nationalist credentials, with influential voices calling for more Chinese military prowess and tougher policies toward the United States, Taiwan, and Japan. Particularly worrisome, even to the CCP, are the so-called *fenqing*—the angry urban youth who express super-chauvinistic views on the Internet. The patriotic education campaigns, which were intended to keep the CCP in power, may ironically contribute to the party's undoing. The particular character of Chinese nationalism propagated by the party, and now by segments of the population, does not lend itself to Chinese acceptance of an American-led world order.

Regime Insecurity. Appeals to nationalism combined with sustained economic growth have fended off mass attempts at regime change since Tiananmen. The CCP, however, is still highly attentive to the work of "foreign and domestic forces" challenging the regime.[39] Though the major powers, to Beijing's great pride, treat China as an equal, under the surface the CCP believes it lives in an inhospitable world. Since the end of the Cold War, the principle of noninterference in the affairs of other countries has given way to more interventions, of both a diplomatic and military character, on behalf of failed states, human rights, and the protection of democracy. For the Chinese leadership, this has not been a welcome development.

Several external shocks have heightened concerns about regime security over the years. Two such shocks were the collapse of the Soviet Union and peaceful demonstrations for democracy across Eastern Europe in places like Poland. These developments eventually gave rise to a new Europe with democratic institutions and market-oriented economies, as well as a strengthening of the North Atlantic Treaty Organization (NATO) that drew these countries closer to the United States and its partners. The erstwhile Soviet Union lost control of its satellite states. Similarly, China fears the loss of what it considers to be its territories, namely Taiwan and Tibet.

A third shock was NATO's humanitarian intervention in Kosovo. If the CCP and the PLA had been awed by U.S. military prowess in the first Gulf War of 1992, at least the war's aims had been to roll back the violation of sovereignty by one country, Iraq, of another, Kuwait. A war to remediate the violation of sovereignty was a principle the CCP could accept. Kosovo represented something entirely different. NATO intervened in the sovereign affairs of another country to stop human rights violations. The anger and angst this caused in Beijing cannot be overstated. What did this mean for the PRC, with all the people it oversaw who wanted their own independence or autonomy? Chinese authors described these actions as efforts by an Anglo-Saxon hegemony to "Christianize" other civilizations and wrote with concern about American hegemony.[40]

Kosovo was just the beginning. European Union nations, the United States, Latin American nations, the Organization of American States, and

Australia have intervened in Georgia, Ukraine, Serbia, Indonesia, Haiti, Liberia, and Slovakia, to name a few, to push for free and fair elections, democracy, and human rights. Despite the fallout from the Iraq war, total European budgets for democracy promotion exceed the U.S. budget.[41] The "democracy norm," or the legitimacy of intervening in a country's sovereign territory to protect human rights, had emerged so strongly that even Kofi Annan, while he was secretary general of the United Nations (UN), announced that sometimes "the responsibility to protect" individual rights trumps state sovereignty.[42] In fact, the UN General Assembly formally adopted the principle at the 2005 World Summit.[43] This represented a terrifying development in international politics for the CCP.

The official *People's Daily* condemned the "democratic offensive" in the former Soviet Union.[44] Hu Jintao warned that "the Soviet Union disintegrated under the assault of their Westernization and bourgeoisie liberalism" and also warned against the dangers lurking from outside sources as exhibited by the "color revolutions" of Georgia and Ukraine.[45] The CCP mapped out a strategy of resistance including a crackdown on Chinese nongovernmental organizations cooperating with their foreign counterparts.

The CCP suspects that the United States was behind these regime changes. Many leaders believe that the United States seeks to contain China and to eventually bring the CCP down as it did the Soviets. Many believe that these polices of containment have accelerated since the United States launched the war on terror. Chinese strategists believe that the United States is "boxing China in" along its periphery, with a presence in Central Asia; partnerships with India, Pakistan, Japan, Korea, and Australia; and increased engagement with Vietnam and the Philippines.[46] They believe America's objective is to prevent "China's influence from rising in the region."[47]

Washington's deployments and increased presence in Central and South Asia and in the Middle East have fueled the Chinese perception of a containment strategy. Though China had initially supported U.S. operations in the region, once the United States began to encourage Central Asian states to undertake political reform and the color revolutions unfolded, China became increasingly suspicious of U.S. intentions.[48]

The CCP has fought back by pushing state sovereignty and non-interference in the affairs of others as sacrosanct principles of international politics. It continues to cozy up to Russia, strengthen the Shanghai Cooperation Organization, and provide support to the world's remaining dictators, such as Karimov, Mugabe, and Chávez.

Criticisms of China's human rights record are viewed and sold to the Chinese public as attempts to embarrass and weaken the PRC. Western leaders' meetings with the Dalai Lama and Uighur activists are met with strong PRC protests. In 2007, China canceled a scheduled U.S. naval port call in Hong Kong after American leaders met with the Dalai Lama. In July 2011, China called on U.S. President Barack Obama to cancel his meeting with the Dalai Lama at the White House, which was not heeded. More recently, Chinese leaders summoned the British ambassador and apparently canceled a visit to Great Britain of a senior Chinese government official after Prime Minister David Cameron met with the spiritual leader in May 2012.[49]

In short, the world is becoming increasingly inhospitable to the CCP as norms governing human rights and democracy promotion are changing and the major powers try to act in accordance with those norms. As a dictatorship with imperial possessions and pretensions, the Chinese communist regime is finding itself increasingly isolated among the major powers.

Chinese "Realism." There is a powerful strain of what Westerners might call "realism" among Chinese elites. In the realist perspective, broadly defined, states must maximize their power to maximize their security. International politics is a competitive, zero-sum game for influence, power, and access to resources. Chinese leaders with this perspective are highly suspicious of calls for China to take more responsibility for upholding an international system that provides collective goods. Countries look out for themselves. This worldview reads "humanitarianism" or the promotion of values as ruses that Westerners, especially Americans, use to maximize their hegemony. Those with this worldview are highly uncomfortable relying upon the U.S. Navy to ensure maritime trade. Chinese realism is reflected in attitudes toward force and keen attentiveness to its relative national power.[50]

Recent work on the history of Chinese warfare has called into question the conventional wisdom that China's Confucian-Mencian tradition made for a peaceful strategic culture.[51] Analysis of the historical record has demonstrated that, like Americans, the Chinese are a martial people. China engaged in 3,790 internal and external wars from 1100 BC to the end of the Qing dynasty in 1911.[52] During the lengthy Ming dynasty (1388–1644), China engaged in an average of 1.12 external wars per year.[53]

This pattern has not ended under the contemporary CCP regime. Since its founding in 1949, the PRC has threatened, used force, or engaged in gunboat diplomacy at least five times in the Taiwan Strait, including twice in the 1990s, in 1950 in Korea against the Americans and their coalition partners, against the Indians in 1962, against the Soviets in 1969, against Vietnam in 1979, in the contested South China Seas throughout the 1990s and today, and in contested waters around Japan in the past few years. In addition, the PRC has probed U.S. naval vessels around Japan and as far away as Guam, has consistently launched cyber-attacks and probes against U.S. assets over the past few years, has lased U.S. satellites, and has conducted the only antisatellite test the world has seen in decades.

While China certainly sees economic growth as an intrinsic good, Chinese nationalists also view growth as a necessary instrument for regaining power and prestige. In the late 1990s, sinologist and defense adviser Michael Pillsbury argued persuasively that China keeps a keen eye on its power status in the world.[54] In fact, Beijing had established specific criteria and formulas to measure its Comprehensive National Power (CNP) against the great powers.[55]

Deng Xiaoping emphasized the importance of measuring CNP to guide needed Chinese reforms. Scoring and measuring CNP is important to assess "the status hierarchy in world politics; the power of potential rivals and potential partners, who will exploit the RMA [revolution in military affairs], which side will win a war, and the trend toward multipolarity and U.S. decline."[56]

Chinese CNP measurements are concerned with the translation of national resources into political power. Both the Chinese Academy of Social Sciences (CASS) and the Academy of Military Science give great weight to "latent" as well as actual power.[57] CASS, for example, divides CNP into natural resources, economic strength, and science and technology.[58]

Chinese CNP indices give great weight to science and technology as keys to twenty-first-century geopolitical power and competition. The CASS index, for example, measures a country's research and development as a proportion of gross domestic product, number of scientists and engineers in absolute terms as well as per 1,000 people, and percentage of high-technology exports as a percentage of total exports.[59]

Chinese leaders are keenly attentive to positions of relative national power and view economic strength as an instrument of national power.[60] They believe, moreover, that the production of a premier science and technology system may be the key to great power status. Many Chinese policymakers, in effect, are not economic liberals thinking about how to maximize national welfare. Rather, they think deeply and systematically about how to maximize China's place in the global system of power, how their science and technology system measures up to other major powers, and most importantly, how innovations in science and technology can advance China's military ambitions.

Other Voices. Despite these troublesome strains in Chinese strategic culture and domestic conditioning of its foreign policy, there are certain hard facts about China's current domestic state that naturally push China to act responsibly. China needs economic growth to maintain social stability—without strong growth, it would be difficult to absorb the continued flow of internal migrants seeking jobs as they move from more rural inland areas to the coast. At least for now, China wants to avoid an open and intense rivalry with the United States and its allies, since that would threaten economic growth.

Some within China's establishment, most prominently Chinese scholar and government adviser Zheng Bijian, argue that their country is striving for "peaceful development" and focusing most of its attention on economic growth and resolving social problems.[61] Zheng argues that China is already deeply embedded in and benefiting from the international system and does not desire to change it. China, he argues, will not follow the path of other rising powers and engage in "rivalry for resources in bloody wars" or, like Germany and Japan before the two world wars, who "violently plundered resources and pursued hegemony."[62] Instead, Zheng argues that China is "strengthening its democratic institutions and the rule of law."[63]

Outside the Chinese political establishment, there are voices for greater justice, moderation, and liberalism. For example, 303 Chinese intellectuals, lawyers, and activists, as well as 10,000 ordinary Chinese citizens, have signed Charter 08, inspired by Charter 77 signed in Czechoslovakia in January 1977. The group called for full freedom and democracy in China and garnered thousands of citizen signatures. The charter includes this statement related to China's foreign policy:

> China, as a major nation of the world, as one of five permanent members of the United Nations Security Council, and as a member of the UN Council on Human Rights, should be contributing to peace for humankind and progress toward human rights. Unfortunately, we stand today as the only country among the major nations that remains mired in authoritarian politics. Our political system continues to produce human rights disasters and social crises, thereby not only constricting China's own development but also limiting the progress of all of human civilization. This must change, truly it must. The democratization of Chinese politics can be put off no longer.[64]

Though many of the charter signers have been arrested, detained, or otherwise harassed, they have been heard; the late Václav Havel, one of the signers of the Czech document, provided his moral support. Liu Xiaobo, one of the document's authors, won the Nobel Peace Prize in 2010. More to the point, not everyone in China accepts the current organization of politics or the direction of Chinese foreign policy.

The arguments of Zheng on the inside of Chinese politics and others on the outside are compelling. Any outside observer can see that China benefits from its participation in the international system, which is why so many Westerners cannot imagine that China will threaten the United States. The PRC, moreover, faces many tough internal challenges, which to an outside observer may seem more important than the pursuit of great power prestige.

As Zheng has written, China still has to grapple with serious developmental challenges:

> The formidable development challenges still facing China stem from the constraints it faces in pulling its population out of

poverty. The scarcity of natural resources available to support such a huge population—especially energy, raw materials, and water—is increasingly an obstacle, especially when the efficiency of use and the rate of recycling of those materials are low. China's per capita water resources are one-fourth of the amount of the world average, and its per capita area of culti-vatable farmland is 40 percent of the world average. China's oil, natural gas, copper, and aluminum resources in per capita terms amount to 8.3 percent, 4.1 percent, 25.5 percent, and 9.7 percent of the respective world averages.[65]

Here Zheng mentions just one domestic challenge: resources. But there are many more such issues, notably including the costs of reform-ing the retirement and pensions system as "China grows old before it grows rich."[66]

Addressing the burden of providing economic security for an aging population will require massive government outlays, along with substan-tial economic and political reforms to build the infrastructure to deliver pensions to the burgeoning retiree population. Yet, this is but one of many such massive and costly problems that China must address—envi-ronmental degradation, the costs of corruption, the instability of massive internal migration, the fragile banking system, an inadequate health care system, and more.

In looking at China's domestic challenges, it is tempting to believe that China will spend most of its time, effort, and money solving them. The optimist logic is persuasive—China has too many problems to become a threat to the United States. It is undeniable that China needs markets and capital. Yet, despite these supposed truisms, much of China's behavior is inconsistent with a purely welfare-maximizing perspective.

Despite greater societal plurality and domestic political pressures, China seems to be pursuing goals consistent with a patient desire to become the dominant Asian-Pacific power. It is quietly countering U.S. influence in the region and throughout the world and pursuing a military buildup to check American advantages.

Conclusion

In sum, while China is undoubtedly a more pluralistic society than it was thirty years ago, pluralism has not led to a Chinese political system that allows for less suspicion of the West. Even though stated U.S. policy and corresponding efforts since the Nixon administration have been designed to bring China into the so-called family of nations, China has not embraced many aspects of the Western-led, post–World War II international order. Domestic politics in China have a dispositive role in shaping China's view that the United States is a rival and that accepting a position as a responsible stakeholder is to be avoided. Nationalism with Chinese characteristics, regime insecurity, and a strong belief in traditional power politics are the forces that now dominate Chinese foreign policy. These three forces are mutually reinforcing: the CCP needs to maximize its power to stay in control, and to do so it stokes a chauvinistic nationalism that perceives the United States as a threat. To fend off threats to its power, the CCP must have a powerful military and exercise its growing power.

These interlinking forces permeate Chinese society. The party leaders making final decisions in China are not all economists or proponents of "rational actor" theories of international behavior. Alongside an increasingly sophisticated technocratic elite sit ardent nationalists and leaders who harbor great ambitions for their country as well as profound grievances that, they believe, must be salved. Despite voices inside and outside of the party who call for greater liberalization for China, the Chinese public has been fed a steady diet of a "victimization narrative" of Chinese history; therefore, many view the United States and other Western powers as antagonists working against their country's growing prosperity and increasing power. Suspicion of the United States has become a part of China's national identity.

Finally, these mutually reinforcing attitudes continue to be manifest in Chinese policy choices and in Chinese responses to U.S. policy. China's military buildup is geared in part toward pushing the United States out of Asia. China has attempted to raise its international standing by characterizing itself as a noninterventionist power. China's drive to increase national prosperity is tied not only to regime insecurity, but also to an effort to grow state power. And finally, China views U.S. policy objectives in Asia as well as U.S. responses to Chinese policy on Taiwan, human rights, and other issues as efforts to contain Chinese power and as affronts to Chinese dignity. This potent combination underpins China's rivalry with the United States and the broader Western-led international system.

Notes

1. Dan Blumenthal and Aaron Friedberg, *An American Strategy for Asia* (Washington, D.C.: American Enterprise Institute, 2009), http://www.aei.org/paper/29144.

2. Much of this section is borrowed from Blumenthal and Friedberg, *An American Strategy for Asia*.

3. See Robert E. Kanet, ed., *A Resurgent Russia and the West: The European Union, NATO, and Beyond* (Dordrecht, The Netherlands: Republic of Letters Publishing, 2009).

4. Blumenthal and Friedberg, *An American Strategy for Asia*.

5. Ohio State University political scientist Alexander Wendt provides a useful definition of rival: "unlike enemies, rivals expect each other to act as if they recognize their sovereignty, their 'life and liberty,' as a *right*, and therefore not to try to conquer or dominate them.... Unlike friends, however, the recognition among rivals does not extend to the right to be free from violence in disputes." See Alexander Wendt, *Social Theory of International Politics* (Cambridge: Cambridge University Press, 1999), 279.

6. Robert B. Zoellick, "Whither China: From Membership to Responsibility?" (presentation to National Committee on U.S.-China Relations, New York, NY, September 21, 2005).

7. Robert B. Zoellick, "From the Shanghai Communiqué to 'Responsible Stakeholder'" (remarks, The China Balance Sheet in 2007 and Beyond, conference, Peterson Institute for International Economics, May 2, 2007), http://www.iie.com/publications/papers/paper.cfm?ResearchID=733.

8. Zoellick, "Whither China."

9. Ibid.

10. Ibid.

11. Ibid.

12. G. John Ikenberry, "The Rise of China and the Future of the West," *Foreign Affairs* 87, no. 1 (2008): 23–37.

13. Ibid. Michael Mandelbaum also argues that the world order is now dominated by "Western ideas" of free markets, democracy, and peaceful resolution of disputes. See Michael Mandelbaum, *The Ideas That Conquered the World: Peace, Democracy, and Free Markets in the Twenty-First Century* (New York: PublicAffairs, 2002).

14. Zoellick, "Whither China."

15. Ibid.

16. Ibid.

17. Ibid.

18. Ong, *China's Security Interests*, 22–33.

19. The conventional wisdom in contemporary political science is finally recognizing what statesmen and classical political scholars like Thucydides and Edmund Burke have always known: that a country's domestic politics significantly influences its external behavior. See the compilation of the social science literature covering domestic influences on foreign policy in Ashley J. Tellis and Michael Wills, eds., *Strategic Asia 2007–08: Domestic Political Change and Grand Strategy* (Seattle & Washington, D.C.: National Bureau of Asian Research, 2007). For a useful survey of how different schools of international relations theory perceive international politics to be enmeshed with domestic politics, see Peter Gourevitch, "The Second Image Reversed: The International Sources of Domestic Politics," *International Organization* 32, no. 4 (1978): 881–912. China scholars such as Bates Gill and Evan S. Medeiros have identified domestic influences on Chinese foreign policy; see, for example, their "Foreign and Domestic Influences on China's Arms Control and Nonproliferation Policies," *The China Quarterly* 161 (March 2000): 66–94. Alistair Ian Johnston and Robert S. Ross include a section on domestic politics in their edited volume on Chinese foreign policy, *New Directions in the Study of China's Foreign Policy* (Palo Alto, CA: Stanford University Press, 2006). Peter Gries has also written extensively on how Chinese nationalism affects its foreign policy. See, for example, Peter Gries, *China's New Nationalism: Pride, Politics, and Diplomacy* (Berkeley and Los Angeles: University of California Press, 2004).

20. David Lampton, *Same Bed, Different Dreams: Managing U.S.-China Relations, 1989–2000* (Berkeley: University of California Press, 2002).

21. Paul A. Papayoanou does a particularly useful service in describing how different interests within Germany and England pushed for either enmity or cooperation. See his "Interdependence, Institutions, and the Balance of Power: Britain, Germany, and World War I," *International Security* 20, no. 4 (1996): 42–76.

22. Minxin Pei, "Political Reform in China: Leadership Differences and Convergence" (Washington, D.C.: Carnegie Endowment for International Peace, 2008), http://www.carnegie-mec.org/publications/?fa=20067.

23. See Jayshree Bajoria, "Nationalism in China," Council on Foreign Relations Backgrounder, April 23, 2008, http://www.cfr.org/china/nationalism-china/p16079.

24. David Shambaugh, "Coping with a Conflicted China," *Washington Quarterly* 34, no. 1 (2011): 7–27.

25. Robert A. Scalapino, "China's Multiple Identities in East Asia: China as a Regional Force," in *China's Quest for National Identity*, ed. Lowell Dittmer and Samuel S. Kim (Ithaca, NY: Cornell University Press, 1993), 217.

26. Ibid., 217.

27. Susan Shirk, *China: Fragile Superpower* (New York: Oxford University Press, 2007), 181–210.

28. Ibid., 36.

29. *Red River Valley* was directed by Xiaoning Feng (FACETS). The film ties Tibet into the "century of humiliation" narrative by telling the story of the British incursion into Tibet. Though little known in the West, *Red River Valley* is popular in China and has won numerous awards.

30. "Profile: Hunting Tigers out in Peking: Chris Patten, Hong Kong's Pugnacious Governor," *The Independent*, January 22, 1994, http://www.independent.co.uk/opinion/profile-hunting-tigers-out-in-peking-chris-patten-hong-kongs-pugnacious-governor-1401670.html.

31. Peter Hays Gries, *China's New Nationalism: Pride, Politics, and Diplomacy* (Berkeley and Los Angeles: University of California Press, 2004), 51.

32. Ibid., 51.

33. Ibid., 34.

34. Peter H. Gries, "Social Psychology and the Identity-Conflict Debate: Is a 'China Threat' Inevitable?" *European Journal of International Relations* 11, no. 2 (2005): 243.

35. Gries, *China's New Nationalism*, 58.

36. Ian Storey and You Ji, "China's Aircraft Carrier Ambitions: Seeking Truth from Rumors," *Naval War College Review* 57, no. 1 (2004): 90–91.

37. Peter H. Gries, "Tears of Rage: Chinese Nationalist Reactions to the Belgrade Embassy Bombing," *China Journal* 46 (2001): 25–43.

38. Deng Yong, "Hegemon on the Offensive: China Perspectives on U.S. Global Strategy," *Political Science Quarterly* 116, no. 3 (2001): 352, quoted in Gries, *China's New Nationalism*, 143.

39. Luo Gan, "Shenru kaizhan shehuihuyi fazhi linian jiaoyu qiueshi jiaqing zhengfa duiwu sixiang zhengzhi jianshe" [Penetratingly carry out education in the concept of the socialist legal system and realistically strengthen the ideological and political construction of the political-legal ranks], *Qiushi zazhi* (December 2006): 3–10, described in Nathan, "China's Political Trajectory," 29; for more on "peaceful evolution," see Ong, *China's Security Interests*, 22–33.

40. June Teufel Dreyer, *China's Political System: Modernization and Tradition*, 5th ed. (New York: Pearson Longman, 2006), 6.

41. Michael McFaul, "Democracy Promotion as a World Value," *Washington Quarterly* 28, no. 1 (2004–2005): 156.

42. Adrian Karatnycky, "The Democratic Imperative," *National Interest* (Summer 2004): 154.

43. United Nations General Assembly, Sixtieth Session, 2005 World Summit Outcome, Resolution 60/253, October 14, 2005, 30.

44. Thomas Carothers, "The Backlash against Democracy Promotion," *Foreign Affairs* 85, no. 2 (2006): 55–68.

45. Shirk, *China: Fragile Superpower,* 47, 38.

46. Mohan Malik, *Dragon on Terrorism: Assessing China's Tactical Gains and Strategic Losses Post September 11,* (Carlisle, PA: Strategic Studies Institute, 2002), 29.

47. Zhai Kun, "What Underlies the U.S.-Philippine Joint Military Exercise," *Beijing Review* (March 14, 2002): 9, quoted in Malik, *Dragon on Terrorism*, 30.

48. Ge Lide, "Will the United States Withdraw from Central and South Asia?" *Beijing Review* (January 17, 2001): 8–9, quoted in Malik, *Dragon on Terrorism*, 29. See also Dan Blumenthal and Joseph Lin, "Oil Obsession: Energy Appetite Fuels Beijing's Plans to Protect Vital Sea Lines," *Armed Forces Journal* (June 2006), http://www.armed forcesjournal.com/2006/06/1813592/. Zhao Nianyu of the State Council–run Shanghai Institute for International Studies pointed to the 2004 Regional Military Security Initiative—a collective security exercise to protect the sea lanes—as a first step by the U.S. military to "garrison the [Malacca] Strait" under the "guise of counterterrorist measures." While Malaysia, Indonesia, and Singapore have taken the lead on patrols, the perception remains in some Chinese circles that "American control" of the straits is a strategic vulnerability. Indonesia and Singapore have declined the U.S. Navy's offer to help patrol the Strait and have instead embarked on a fairly successful multilateral effort themselves. Thus, China's fears of U.S. control of the Strait of Malacca are not well founded.

49. See the following articles: Maureen Fan, "China's Naval Rebuff Could Be Reply to Dalai Lama's Medal," *Washington Post*, November 24, 2007; "Barack Obama meets the Dalai Lama at the White House," *Associated Press*, July 16, 2011; Tania Branigan, "China cancels UK visit over David Cameron's meeting with Dalai Lama," *The Guardian*, May 25, 2012.

50. On particular Chinese interpretations of a competitive political environment see Dan Blumenthal, "What Happened to China's 'Peaceful Rise'?" *Foreign Policy*, October 21, 2010, http://shadow.foreignpolicy.com/posts/2010/10/21/what_happened_to_chinas_peaceful_rise.

51. For a summary of this argument, see Alastair Iain Johnston, *Cultural Realism: Strategic Culture and Grand Strategy in Chinese History* (Princeton, NJ: Princeton University Press, 1995), 63–65.

52. Johnston, *Cultural Realism*, 27.

53. Ibid.

54. Michael Pillsbury, *China Debates the Future Security Environment* (Washington, D.C.: National Defense University Press, 2000).

55. Ibid., 203–205.

56. Ibid., 256–57.

57. Ibid., 219–25.

58. Ibid., 219–22 .

59. Ibid., 221.

60. David M. Lampton, *The Three Faces of Chinese Power: Might, Money, and Minds* (Berkeley and Los Angeles: University of California Press, 2008), 20–25.

61. Zheng Bijian, "The 16th National Congress of the Communist Party of China and China's Peaceful Rise—A New Path" (speech, Center for Strategic

and International Studies, Washington, D.C., December 9, 2002); Zheng Bijian, "A New Path for China's Peaceful Rise and the Future of Asia" (speech, Bo'ao Forum for Asia, Boao, Hainan, China, November 3, 2003); Zheng Bijian, "China's Peaceful Rise and Opportunities for the Asia-Pacific Region" (speech, Roundtable Meeting between the Bo'ao Forum for Asia and the China Reform Forum, Boao, Hainan, China, April 18, 2004).

62. Zheng Bijian, "China's 'Peaceful Rise' to Great-Power Status," *Foreign Affairs* 84, no. 5 (September/October 2005): 18–24.

63. Ibid.

64. Perry Link, "China's Charter 08," *New York Review of Books* 56, no. 1 (January 15, 2009). See also Sharon Hom and Stacy Mosher, eds., *Challenging China: Struggle and Hope in an Era of Change* (New York: New Press, 2008), for a compilation of essays by the many scholars and activists calling for greater liberalization within China.

65. Zheng, "China's 'Peaceful Rise,'" 19.

66. Isabel Hilton, "China May Grow Old before It Grows Rich," *Guardian*, April 28, 2011, http://www.guardian.co.uk/commentisfree/2011/apr/28/china-ageing-population-migrant-labourers.

2

The U.S.-China Relationship: A Security Analyst's Assessment

Dan Blumenthal

In the international political arena, China continues to reject the invitation to become a responsible stakeholder. Rather than contribute to the stability of the international system from which it benefits, Chinese policies often have the converse effect. Indeed, China appears to be attempting to remake its external environment to suit its own interests. Unhappily, those interests clash with those of the United States and most other Asian states.

There are both military and political indicators that China has adopted the role of an irresponsible actor and is behaving as a rival to the United States. Its military buildup, which has been largely designed with a potential American adversary in mind, is destabilizing to the region. Beijing's attitude toward Asian regional institutions is more exclusive of other powers than inclusive, pointing to a Chinese desire to dominate its neighborhood. Its imperial approach to dealing with internal ethnic minorities portends a heavy-handed, aggressive approach to external relations. Finally, China has been unhelpful, if not outright disruptive, on matters that should concern all nations such as North Korean nuclearization.

The Military Indicators of Rival Behavior

Unlike past rising powers, and particularly in contrast with the Soviets, whose demise China studies seriously,[1] China wisely decided to invest resources in its military gradually and incrementally. There is no "smoking gun" document that describes a grand Chinese plan for regional or global dominance, but observation of Chinese behavior makes clear the contours of a Chinese national strategy based on devoting considerable resources generated by China's prodigious growth to building what it calls Comprehensive National Power (CNP). At the same time, through "good neighbor" policies, China parries attempts by other powers to contain it while asserting itself diplomatically.[2]

China has invested in a serious military and has grown impressively in both economic might and diplomatic stature. China's military buildup has been gradual, but even the PLA's incremental approach to military modernization has yielded substantial dividends. While other major powers were slashing their defense budgets, the PLA's average budgetary growth of over 10 percent per year has driven the largest military buildup in the post–Cold War era.[3]

China's military is perhaps the greatest evidence of an emerging Sino-American rivalry, or at least China's view of the United States as a rival. It cannot be explained by external threats. Indeed, since the collapse of the Soviet Union, China has faced one of the more peaceful environments in its history. Yet, since the early 1990s the PRC has devoted a meaningful portion of its growing wealth to military modernization even in the face of massive social needs.

If external threats do not justify this military modernization program, what does? The first driver of the PRC buildup is nationalism. The CCP believes that "national greatness" requires a strong military.[4] For example, a strong military is needed to take back Taiwan, even if faced with Japanese and U.S. resistance, thereby righting a supposed historical wrong committed against China. Like all irredentist claims, China's interest in annexing Taiwan is not primarily about the actual security of the PRC. Taiwan poses no material threat to China, and China would gain no economic advantage and only a limited security advantage from retaking Taiwan. To the contrary, the economic relationship with Taiwan has been an important driver of China's growth. The PRC's commitment to developing capabilities for conflict with the United States, Japan, and Taiwan is a result of nationalistic fervor. But, as noted China scholar David Shambaugh has written, "Yet China's military modernization cannot be explained by Taiwan contingencies alone."[5] Professor David Lai concurs that Beijing also wants a military "commensurate with its international status" that can cope with regional disputes over territory, respond to America's overwhelming presence along its periphery, and, over time, protect its own energy supplies.[6]

The second driver of the military buildup is regime insecurity. Since the shock of Tiananmen, the military has arguably grown in importance to the PRC. The PLA and the internal security forces are the ultimate guarantors of CCP rule. Chinese leaders believe in the need for a strong PLA to keep the country together and to beat down "splittist threats" from foreign forces and within Tibet and Xinjiang.[7] The PLA must also defend against the perceived hostile Americans and their Western allies, who, many Chinese appear to believe, are trying to bring down the CCP and contain China.[8]

The third driver is a demonstrable belief in the efficacy of force and the importance of military power in international politics. Chinese leaders, unlike their counterparts in contemporary Europe, for example, believe that the use of force is still decisive in international politics. A fairly prominent spokesman for a more hawkish national security policy is PLA Navy rear admiral Yang Yi, who argues for a larger defense budget so that China can protect its increasing international investments, citizens abroad, and energy supply routes as well as defeat U.S. forces coming to the defense of Taiwan.[9]

Authors of China's 2006 Defense White Paper also raise concerns about resources and transportation links when they state that "security issues related to energy, resources, finance, information, and international shipping routes are mounting."[10] The CCP has expressed a desire to protect energy investments in Central Asia and land lines of communication that lead there. This would require new types of military investment. Ongoing disagreements with Japan over maritime claims in the East China Sea—once simply fodder for PLA writers—have sparked naval incidents and economic embargoes, with the potential for further confrontation.[11] Similar disputes with several Southeast Asian claimants to all or parts of the Spratly and Paracel Islands in the South China Sea could lead as well to renewed tensions or conflict.[12] China has also deployed more troops to the Korean border and begun to plan for intervention in the Korean Peninsula in a crisis in order to secure its borders and perhaps even to secure loose nuclear weapons and materials.[13]

Many argue that all great powers have great militaries. This argument is true to a point, but largely irrelevant. In the twenty-first century, most great powers have de-emphasized the need for strong military capabilities and the use of force. Most of today's major powers are highly ambivalent about the utility of military power. For example, Japan is still relatively pacifist despite increasing threats from the PRC and North Korea. The Japanese have not increased their defense budget[14] and have reacted relatively mildly to Chinese incursions, such as the incident in September 2010 that resulted in Japan meekly releasing the captain of a Chinese fishing vessel that had intruded into Japanese-controlled waters under dispute with China and Taiwan. The EU countries no longer define greatness in terms of military power and have been deaf to American urging to increase their defense spending.[15]

Moreover, it is the *character* rather than the mere fact of a military modernization program that matters. The recent surge of military spending by the United States mostly has been used to prosecute the "long war" against jihadi radicals, a fight that benefits all states in the liberal order. China has not built up its forces to combat terror groups or to contribute to military operations that maintain the international system.

It is unclear what the PRC intends to do with all of this military power. But the United States, as the guarantor of international security, must infer Chinese intentions from capabilities. The PLA is deploying, testing, and training its new military capabilities as though it views the United States and U.S. allies and partners as adversaries.[16] The PLA has focused on acquiring capabilities designed to take advantage of key perceived U.S. weaknesses, including America's distance from the Asia-Pacific, its reliance on allied and friendly bases and ports to project military power, and its reliance on space- and terrestrial-based information systems to conduct military operations.[17] All of China's military services have been expanded and modernized. The extent of China's attention to and the nature of its military modernization reflect its view of the United States as its rival.

Scope of the Buildup. China has been engaged in an across-the-board force modernization. Among the key benefactors of Beijing's large defense investments, due to their central role in China's evolving military strategy, are its aerospace forces. The PLA's second artillery, or strategic and missile force, has been adding ballistic and cruise missiles to its arsenal more rapidly than any other military. Since the end of the Cold War, the stock of cruise and ballistic missiles placed opposite Taiwan has grown substantially. Public estimates vary from 1,000 to 1,600. There was increasing speculation in 2010 that it would reach 1,900 or 2,000 by the end of that year.[18] As a consequence, Taiwan now faces the most daunting missile threat in the world. But it is not just Taiwan that must contend with this threat. The PLA has created new missile units with conventional theater-range missiles, deployed at various locations in China and useful in a variety of contingencies. These missiles can only be used for offensive purposes. They put U.S. and allied fixed air bases in Japan and South Korea well within range of Chinese military power. And the PLA is developing ballistic missiles whose purpose is to hit mobile maritime assets coming toward China from the Pacific.

China's quickly modernizing nuclear weapons and strategic weapons programs provide it with another coercive capability. New classes and variants of intercontinental and submarine-launched ballistic missiles can hit the American continent with nuclear weapons. No other country is adding to its strategic arsenal so quickly. While Chinese doctrine dictates that nuclear weapons are to be used only in retaliation, the ongoing modernization of the program and the missiles that would deliver the weapons has changed the calculus of power in the region. By the end of the decade, China will possess a modern nuclear arsenal of several hundred warheads. China's missiles have provided it with a serious power-projection capability.

The PLA's air force has been likewise adding modern fighter aircraft to its arsenal more quickly than any other military. From 2000 to 2011, the PLA's air force grew from roughly 65 fourth-generation aircraft to roughly 480 (including J-10s, J-11s, and Su-30s)[19] Acquisition of unmanned aerial vehicles, such as Harpy drones from Israel, has provided the Chinese air force with capabilities to strike enemy air defenses from the air at longer ranges.[20] China's air force can strike at Taiwan as well as at U.S. and allied bases in Japan and South Korea. Airborne early-warning and aerial-refueling programs will allow the PRC to conduct air operations in the South China Sea, where it aims to enforce its still-disputed territorial claims.

With air and missile forces, China today has the ability to establish air superiority over the Taiwan Strait and possibly over Japan. If China's air force continues to grow as it did over the past decade, it could have as many as 1,000 modern fighter aircraft, by far the most in the Pacific, within the next decade.

China's maritime power has been similarly growing by leaps and bounds. No country has been building, buying, and deploying submarines at the pace of China. Between 2002 and 2004, the military deployed thirteen submarines: One KILO-class diesel-powered submarine delivered from Russia and the indigenously produced SONG class.[21] It is the only country in the world with five ongoing diesel electric submarine programs.

Assuming a steady rate of submarine commissioning and a submarine lifespan of twenty to thirty years, China could have up to eighty-five subs of all kinds within the next decade. One would have to go back to the interwar period to find a comparable level of submarine deployment. China is estimated to have two *Jin* class ballistic missiles in its nuclear force, with three additional hulls awaiting commission. The capability level is unknown, but each of these new subs will carry twelve nuclear-armed JL-2 submarine-launched ballistic missiles, which could reach initial operational capability in the next several years.

In addition, China has a fleet of some seventy surface combatants.[22] China has built or acquired at least four or five *classes* of naval destroyers since 1990.[23] Within the next decade, China's fleets of modern submarines and surface combatants could expand by 10 percent.[24] That would make it the greatest naval power in the region.

China's leaders are also moving forward with an aircraft carrier program, starting with the use of a former Soviet Kuznetsov-class aircraft carrier as a platform for training purposes. China is also looking to outfit its aircraft carriers with fighters, including indigenously produced J-15s. The ex-*Varyag*, which the Chinese purchased from Ukraine, embarked on its initial test voyage in 2011, and it is speculated that it will carry J-15s.

China's new naval capabilities can already contest the U.S. military in the seas surrounding Taiwan and Japan. China's submarines and destroyers, equipped with advanced antiship cruise missiles and advanced undersea mining capability, make the prospect of a U.S. carrier battle group entering the waters surrounding Taiwan and Japan potentially deadly. In addition,

China is seeking the capacity to put allied surface ships at risk in what is referred to as "the second island chain," which extends from Japan to Guam and beyond in the Western Pacific.[25] These are geographic areas where the U.S. military has enjoyed freedom of action and security since the end of World War II. American freedom of action has enabled the U.S. military to deter threats, defend allies, and generally act as Asia's great stabilizer.

In addition to deploying capabilities to attack U.S. assets in the Asia-Pacific, China is developing indirect means for countering U.S. forces. The PLA believes that under certain conditions, an inferior force can defeat a superior force.[26] The key to this strategy is the ability to take advantage of a perceived key weakness of the Americans: their dependence on information technology on the ground and in space for intelligence, reconnaissance, surveillance, and command and control.

The PLA believes that it can defeat U.S. forces by blinding and deafening them, which helps to explain Beijing's ambitious drive to obtain space and cyberwarfare capabilities, to probe American cybernetworks, and to test antisatellite technology. In these areas, the PLA appears to be quite successful. The January 11, 2007, antisatellite test is a case in point. Using a mobile platform, the PLA launched a two-staged solid-fueled missile carrying a kinetic kill vehicle that slammed into a Chinese weather satellite in low earth orbit. By any measure, this was a serious military development.[27] As Chinese analyst Wang Hucheng has indicated, American dependence on space constitutes the "U.S. military's 'soft ribs' and 'strategic weakness.'"[28] Countries cannot win a war against the United States "using the method of tanks and planes," so attacking the U.S. space system "may be an irresistible" option. He explains, "Part of the reason is that the Pentagon is greatly dependent on space" for military operations.[29]

China is also one of the world's most active initiators of cyberattacks and penetration against U.S. government and business information systems. China's "cybermilitias," government-associated hackers, have penetrated U.S. systems to steal private business information, conduct espionage, and generally harass perceived enemies of China.[30] Consistent with its view of the United States as a rival, China has created a sophisticated means to gain sensitive information about its potential adversary, to obtain a competitive business advantage for its companies, and to prepare for a potential war involving cyberattacks.

As more capabilities of all varieties come on line, the CCP has not hesitated to exercise them, sometimes in "gunboat diplomacy" demonstrations meant to intimidate U.S. regional allies. In the 1990s, the PRC engaged in military muscle-flexing in disputed territories in the South China Sea. China and Vietnam had naval contretemps in 1992 and 1994; the Chinese navy seized Mischief Reef from the Philippines in February 1995; and Chinese shows of force in the South China Sea continued into the late 1990s.

Recently, China has once again become more aggressive in asserting its claims in the South China Sea. In March 2009, the Chinese navy repeatedly harassed the U.S. naval ship *Impeccable* while it was unarmed on a mission monitoring submarine activity. China demanded that the United States cease surveillance missions off its coast, despite the fact that the *Impeccable* was operating in international waters.[31] There was also a string of incidents in 2011. Chinese naval and patrol vessels fired warning shots at fishing boats in disputed territory and rammed and cut survey cables of PetroVietnam vessels in Vietnam's Exclusive Economic Zone. Two fighter jets, purported to be Chinese, were spotted near the Philippines's Palawan Island in May. Most recently, China and the Philippines engaged in a lengthy stand-off near the Scarborough Shoal, with China deploying paramilitary vessels against the much weaker Philippines.[32]

China has cast its ravenous gaze eastward as well. Under Hu's watch, during what is supposed to be a period of "peaceful development," the PRC has deployed naval power to disputed areas of the East China Sea, used its submarines to probe the waters in and around Japan, and even surfaced a submarine very close to an American carrier.[33]

In January 2005, Japan spotted two Chinese navy missile-equipped destroyers in the waters near the Japan-China median line, cruising toward an ocean survey vessel chartered by Japan.[34] Later that year, Japanese intelligence detected a flotilla of Chinese warships near a Chinese gas rig "exploiting resources in the East China Sea that are claimed by Japan."[35] The East China Sea was also the location of two of China's largest joint military exercises, including joint naval and air force exercises with Russia in August 2005.[36]

In September 2010, China escalated a longstanding maritime row with with Japan when a Chinese trawler rammed into two Japanese coast guard vessels near the disputed Senkaku/Diaoyutai Islands. Beijing quickly cut off ministerial-level channels to Japan as well as rare-earth exports, a resource Japan depends on China to supply. China also held four Japanese nationals in custody, accusing them of spying, until the captain of the detained vessel was released; Beijing then demanded an apology.

The Purposes and Future of Chinese Military Power. China, as James Holmes and Toshi Yoshihara have documented, has begun an important internal debate about the necessity of sea control for a nation reliant on foreign commerce. Officers writing in Chinese military journals speak in Mahanian terms popular in nineteenth-century America, Britain, and Germany: "[he] who controls the seas controls the world;"[37] "the command of communications on the sea" is "vital for the future and destiny of the nation;"[38] and:

> "it is extremely risky for a major power such as China to become overly dependent on foreign import without adequate protection," and thus China needed to "build up our navy as quickly as possible" in preparation for the "sea battle" that was the ultimate way seafaring nations resolve economic disputes.[39]

An overwhelming reliance on Middle Eastern suppliers has exacerbated Chinese anxiety over energy security. In particular, U.S. naval control of regional sea lines of communication, through which most of Beijing's crude oil passes, is seen as a troubling vulnerability.[40] The fact that over 60 percent of the PRC's oil imports pass through the Straits of Malacca has caused particular alarm in the Chinese media, which refers to it as the "Malacca dilemma."[41] There is only one adversary against whom China must protect itself: the United States.[42]

Chinese military authors and other officers write that China cannot be a great power if it does not have the ability to project military power and protect its international interests.[43] A strong military is needed to defend the PRC again from humiliation and the imposition of the will of hostile powers. Yet, many countries have long supply routes through which their commercial shipping must travel, but few besides China are building their own power-projection capabilities.

Already the PRC appears to be building the capacity to attack American surface ships as far away as Guam, which would be the first time since World War II that American ships in the Pacific were at risk so close to U.S. territory. As China improves its capabilities in command, control, communications, computers, intelligence, reconnaissance, and surveillance (C4ISR), including space-based and over-the-horizon sensors, Beijing will be able to identify, track, and target military activities deep into the western Pacific Ocean.

China's deployment of these capabilities in the last decade has changed the regional balance of power. In 1996, the United States could send a carrier battle group to the waters around Taiwan with impunity in response to a Chinese missile test.[44] That is no longer the case. What is more, while these Chinese capabilities are geared toward a Taiwan contingency, they can be employed to keep the United States out of other regional contingencies as well.

In short, the PRC peacetime military buildup is a strong indication that China sees the United States as a rival. No actual threat to China justifies the buildup. It is driven by nationalist fervor, a perception of Western hostility, and a belief that a nation's military is the ultimate arbiter of international politics.

In analyzing China's military advancement, the Department of Defense proclaimed in its Quadrennial Defense Review (QDR) that of all major and emerging powers, China "has the greatest potential to compete militarily with the United States and field disruptive military technologies that could over time offset traditional U.S. military advantages absent U.S. counterstrategies."[45] In particular, U.S. policymakers are concerned that

> China is likely to continue making large investments in high-end asymmetric military capabilities, emphasizing electronic and cyber-warfare; counter-space operations; ballistic and cruise missiles; advanced integrated air defense systems; next generation torpedoes; advanced submarines; strategic nuclear strike from modern, sophisticated land- and sea-based systems; and theater unmanned aerial vehicles for employment by the Chinese military.[46]

The QDR goes on to say that "these capabilities, the vast distances of the Asian theater, China's continental depth, and the challenge of en route and in-theater U.S. basing" pose serious challenges to America's strategy of providing security and maintaining regional order.[47]

The U.S. military has a host of strategic tasks in the Asia-Pacific: to defend and reassure allies, to address incidents of proliferation, and generally to provide the security umbrella within which Asian countries can continue to prosper. China's military modernization enables it to coerce or even to attack many of these Asian allies. Washington must plan to defend against many possible Chinese uses of force.

Moreover, given uncertainties as to where and when threats may emerge, America's defense strategy is to "secure strategic access and retain global freedom of action."[48] Before 9/11 the United States did not expect to be fighting a long land war in Afghanistan. To do so, it needed to access Eurasia quickly and without opposition. China is developing capabilities that it may use to restrict U.S. access to countries housing U.S. enemies or to extract high costs in return for access. The United States is less safe as a consequence. China is the only country developing capabilities that could prevent or restrict America's "global freedom of action."

The PRC is working to check Washington's ability to project power in the region, a change that is destabilizing. If China succeeds, what alternative will it provide to U.S. military primacy? It does not seem likely that the PRC is ready or willing to provide the public goods now provided by the U.S. military. And it seems even less likely that the Asian nations will accept the CCP as their security guarantor.

The Political Indicators of Rival Behavior

China's implicit rejection of the invitation to be a responsible stakeholder is evident not only in its armed forces modernization, but also in its political behavior. While it develops military capabilities to hold U.S. forces out of Asian waters, it simultaneously launches diplomatic initiatives to exclude Washington from the region's affairs. It also has countered U.S. efforts to solve problems, such as North Korea's nuclearization, that threaten all countries in the region. Beijing's means for dealing with Taiwan and with domestic ethnic minority "splittists" are also revealing. It points to a country that prefers a heavy hand to negotiations and prefers to quash problems rather than address them. All told, Beijing's political behavior suggests a China that will be more difficult to deal with in the years ahead.

Asian Multinational Organizations. Since the late 1990s, China has changed its attitude and embraced regional multilateral forums. It used to view multilateral gatherings as hostile attempts to contain it. But now China sees the utility of not only participating in Asian forums but in creating new ones as well. Its clear preference is for forums that exclude the United States and minimize the importance of U.S. allies. Beijing's change in approach may serve two Chinese purposes. First, it can reassure neighbors that its intentions are peaceful rather than threatening. Second, it can diminish U.S. influence in the region.

Beijing is paying particular attention to two institutions: the Shanghai Cooperation Organization (SCO) and the East Asia Summit. The SCO has previously "requested" that U.S. troops depart Central Asia and is beginning to take on the color of a counterweight to U.S. power.[49] Recent SCO statements provide subtle indications that American goals do not align with those of SCO members. In a 2009 speech on Afghanistan, SCO Secretary General Bolat Nurgaliev stated that Afghanistan needed "stability, not transformation from the outside" to prosper.[50] Several American analysts, including Stephen Blank of the U.S. Army War College, have noted that SCO statements about external interference in Central Asia are "euphemism[s] used to describe Washington's calls for increased democratization in Central Asia."[51] Regarding China specifically, their greatest fear has been that American involvement in Central Asia means American activity on their borders, especially near unstable regions such as Xinjiang. This plays into China's fear of "encirclement."

The story of the East Asia Summit also reveals much about Beijing's attitude toward regional institutions. The summit was first proposed by Malaysia in the early 1990s as an Asian-only forum; the United States and its allies counterproposed the Asia-Pacific Economic Cooperation (APEC), which included many of Washington's democratic allies, including Taiwan. For obvious reasons, the PRC has never much liked APEC as a vehicle for increased regional integration. Instead, it backed the Association of Southeast Asian Nations Plus 3 (China, Japan, and South Korea), confident that with a still-simmering Japanese–South Korean rivalry, it had nothing to fear from America's allies. Beijing also backed an East Asia Summit as an alternative to APEC but then became less supportive when Japan and other U.S. allies lobbied hard for Indian and Australian inclusion over Chinese objections. Chinese official newspapers decried the Japanese for bringing in countries that were not really Asian, that would bring up human rights issues, and that would be American stooges.

When it comes to Asian regionalism, China is not really integrating into existing frameworks. Rather, it is either shaping institutions to serve its own power-political purposes or picking and choosing ones that dilute U.S. influence and avoid Chinese weaknesses such as human rights and democracy. This policy can be explained by China's desire to diminish the influence of a perceived hostile United States and by its view that it should be the leader of Asia.

"Splittism." The CCP is offended, even threatened, by the notion that other countries judge China by its behavior in what it deems to be its domestic politics.[52] For example, Sino-American friction arguably reaches its highest pitch when U.S. presidents meet the Dalai Lama. Established powers are more skeptical of China's rise when they see China's human rights abuses at home. The world watches as China continues its military coercion of Taiwan. And China's commitment to its stated goals of "peaceful development" can be measured by how it deals with its manifold social and economic challenges.

Responsible great powers in the twenty-first century address issues of ethnic or national tensions and separatism peacefully and through democratic processes. For example, Canada has twice allowed Quebec to hold a referendum on separation from the rest of Canada. In modern democratic states, minority rights are protected, and consequently past problems of separatism mostly recede. In contrast, China's approach to its minorities is inconsistent with peaceful development and the actions of a responsible power.

On the issue of separatism, the nationalistic forces in China dominate policy. The CCP has linked its own legitimacy to its ability to fend off "splittism" and hold on to the Chinese empire.[53] Much of what Beijing calls "One China" does not want to be part of One China; at the least, many Uighurs, Tibetans, Mongolians, and Hong Kongers want more autonomy and respect for their distinct ethnic, national, and religious identities. Many Taiwanese, of course, already consider Taiwan as separate from the PRC. As China scholar Ross Terrill has argued, China is the last remaining multicultural empire, holding on to lands conquered over the last two centuries.[54] The CCP has not only made it a high priority to hold on to territories dominated by aggrieved minorities, but it has also set about reclaiming "lost territories" such as Hong Kong, Macau, and, it hopes eventually, Taiwan. Fending off "splittism" and reclaiming lost territory are fundamental CCP objectives. Largely as a result of CCP propaganda, these policies are immensely popular among many Chinese.[55]

The reality of an imperial and aggressive China that represses the rights of its minorities and threatens to annex territory forcefully, undermines the CCP's stated goal to rise "peacefully." One would assume that Chinese policymakers who tend toward a policy of "peaceful development" would argue for a softer approach in Tibet, Xinjiang, Hong Kong, and Taiwan. Some outside the system have; for example, a group of Chinese intellectuals called upon the CCP to stop its 2008 crackdown in Tibet.[56]

But those who call for a different approach tend to lose the argument. Whenever China faces such a choice, it chooses to use a heavy hand against "splittists" rather than adopting policies more consistent with "peaceful development" and the desire to be regarded as a responsible twenty-first century power. The most important examples are Beijing's treatment of Tibet and Xinjiang.

Tibet. Beijing has made that choice repeatedly in Tibet, which always has the potential for unrest. Since China's conquest of Tibet in 1959, Beijing has used a multifaceted policy of flooding the region with Han Chinese and promoting economic growth.[57] At the same time, it vilifies the Dalai Lama and refuses to concede more autonomy for the region. During the six-year tenure of Zhang Qingli, fresh from his duties crushing dissent in Xinjiang, as Communist Party Secretary in Tibet, the region was a tinderbox.

Zhang enforced rules banning students and civil servants and their families from taking part in religious activities, stepped up invective against the revered Dalai Lama, and urged more "patriotic re-education" campaigns throughout Tibet.[58] It was thus no great surprise that on March 10, 2008, the anniversary of the 1959 Tibetan uprising against the CCP and the fleeing of the Dalai Lama, Tibetans launched a protest. Tibetans, including monks, protested, sometimes violently, against CCP repression and perceived Han Chinese privileges. These protests took place in monasteries and on the streets. The Chinese imposed a news blackout, but reports from journalists inside Tibet indicated that demonstrations spread from Lhasa's main monasteries to monasteries in Gansu, Sichuan, and Qinghai provinces.[59]

The appointment in August 2011 of Chen Quanguo as CCP Party Secretary of Tibet has not brought about any significant changes to the situation. Chen did not come into the job with a reputation as a hardliner, but he still carries out the policies of the central government through various types of repression. In January 2012, for example, Chen announced that monasteries would come under direct rule of the government with party officials stationed at monasteries all over Tibet. This ended the previous policy allowing Tibetans to manage their monestaries autonomously so long as they abide by government regulations.[60] Self immolations protesting repressive government policies have continued under his rule. There are few indications that the situation will improve.

On top of their grievances against the CCP for cultural and religious repression, many Tibetans believe that Han Chinese receive preferential economic and political treatment. The protests reflected anger over both. Like any country would, China had to restore order to Tibet and stop violent rioting. But after gaining control over the riots, rather than addressing the many real Tibetan grievances—and despite international outrage, the risk of an Olympic boycott, and the damage to China's reputation—the CCP chose a strategy that included vilifying the "Dalai clique" (the Dalai Lama and those who support him), mass arrests without due process, a media clampdown, and stoking the flames of popular nationalism by portraying legitimate international outrage as yet another attempt by the "West" to embarrass China. In short, it chose to continue its imperial policy toward Tibet.

Xinjiang. As in Tibet, China has followed a colonization policy in Xinjiang, encouraging a large migration of Han Chinese; diluting local culture, language, and traditions; and restricting the practice of religion, all while committing resources to the province's economic growth. Xinjiang is home to millions of Muslims, most of Turkic ethnicity, and is rich in important oil and gas resources. The region also provides access to Central Asian oil and gas. The CCP conquered Xinjiang and considers it part of "One China," but most Uighurs do not want any part of the PRC.

The transfer of ethnic Chinese labor has exacerbated political tensions. As one would predict, Xinjiang locals abhorred the mass immigration of strangers, and many of the economic gains of investment were unevenly distributed, favoring the Han segment of the population. As in Tibet, Uighurs felt increasingly marginalized in their traditional homeland.

These tensions became evident in February 1997 when a number of residents of Yining staged a demonstration. They protested Chinese restrictions on religious and cultural activities, the migration of Chinese settlers to the region, and the perceived economic and social privileges of the Han.[61]

Again the CCP faced a choice. One would assume that the "peaceful development" school would address the many real grievances of the Uighurs. The Uighur protest was, after all, peaceful. But the nationalists prevailed. The security forces, composed of the Public Security Bureau and the People's Armed Police, brutally put down the protest and shot a number of unarmed demonstrators and arrested thousands of Uighurs. The government also instituted policies targeting religion as a source of opposition. Mosques and religious schools were closed.[62] More than 1 million troops were stationed in the region as a warning to Xinjiang's Uighurs.[63]

Beijing's "strike hard" policies against Xinjiang got a further boost after the 9/11 attacks on the United States. For the first time, the CCP asserted that opposition in Xinjiang was connected to international terrorism, including Osama bin Laden himself. Other great powers would have sympathy for a China that truly faced a threat from jihadists. But that does not appear to be the case in Xinjiang, where alleged links to bin Laden and al Qaeda have been tenuous at best. Instead, China continues to follow repressive policies toward its Uighur population, motivated by its desire to keep control over Xinjiang. When presented with a choice between cracking down or choosing to grant Uighurs more autonomy and respect for religious practices, China has invariably chosen the former. Unlike other powers such as Canada or England, the CCP treats its minorities as colonial subjects and separatists who are enemies of "One China."

Taiwan. China has likewise used a heavy hand in its dealings with Taiwan. Ever since Taiwan's first presidential election in 1995, China has embarked on a predominantly coercive policy toward what it considers the last holdout of imperial China. But while the military is the primary tool of the PRC's Taiwan policy, it is not China's only tool. Beijing has embarked on an energetic diplomatic offensive to convince other states to reverse their diplomatic recognition of Taiwan and to exclude Taiwan from international organizations, even those where sovereignty is not a prerequisite for membership.[64]

The election and subsequent re-election of a more conciliatory Taiwanese president would appear to offer the Chinese a great opportunity to soften their stance on Taiwan. Even after the March 2008 election, however, China's approach to Taiwan has remained much more reliant on sticks than on carrots. There is no indication that China will pare down its military forces. And while China did not deny Taiwan's bid for observership status in the World Health Organization in May 2009, there appears to be little prospect that Beijing will acquiesce to greater involvement in other international organizations for Taiwan. Rather, as China continues to modernize its military and double down on its revanchist ambitions, Taiwan's future freedom is increasingly in doubt. The question remains whether China will take the ultimate and more costly step of actually using its impressive military to bring back this last holdout.

China's Relations with Rogue Regimes: The Case of North Korea. Given its nuclear weapons program, its habitual proliferation, and its recurring aggressive acts, North Korea poses real threats to both regional stability and global security. Thanks to its status as North Korea's only friend and ally, China could play a constructive role in mitigating those threats. And indeed, China has hosted the six-party talks to denuclearize North Korea. But it has proved unwilling to exert any consequential pressure on North Korea. In fact, in 2010 alone, China accounted for

80 percent of North Korea's trade, and bilateral trade between the two reached $1.3 billion, thus undercutting any effect sanctions would have to persuade Pyongyang.[65] The United States expected China not only to use its considerable leverage to press for the abandonment of nuclear weapons, but also to press for economic and political reform on the peninsula. Yet, for two decades, China has failed to use the tools, primarily economic, at its disposal to do so.

In May 2010, China sided with Pyongyang following the *Cheonan* sinking, in which a North Korean torpedo killed forty-six South Korean sailors. Not only did Beijing fail to condemn Pyongyang's behavior, but it attempted to prevent U.S. naval exercises in the Yellow Sea and, in reaction, conducted its own exercises as a deterrent for future U.S.-South Korean drills. This is the height of irresponsibility. The expectation of a responsible stakeholder is to strengthen the system from which it benefits. Now China has in essence allowed a nuclear, unstable regime to maintain power and to threaten the stability of the region with blatant acts of war.

Conclusion

The complexities of analyzing and making policy toward China are manifold. American interaction with China is deep and multidimensional. There is little doubt that the United States has benefited from trade with China and from China's decision to dispose of Maoism. The economists who tend toward a positive sum worldview have, for the most part, carried the day in America's China policy debate. But while economists have a strong argument for why Beijing *should* reform itself into an advanced industrial democracy, it is simply not doing so.

As discussed in the previous chapter, the forces within China that push its foreign policy toward rivalry with the United States appear to dominate the discussions among Chinese decision makers. These forces are mutually reinforcing—an aggrieved nationalism, regime insecurity, and a "realist" or "power-political" view of international politics. The regime can also stay in power because, alongside economic growth, the public views it as the sole vessel through which China can restore the preeminent status that it lost centuries ago.

The nature of the Chinese system prohibits open foreign policy debates where hawks and doves or liberals, populists, and conservatives can be identified. Occasionally, authors, protesters, public intellectuals, dissidents, and PLA officers take public positions, but how much influence they have over the nine "deciders" who comprise the Standing Committee of the CCP Politburo is almost impossible to discern. The opacity of the system leads the United States and its allies to infer intentions from growing capabilities and exercises of power. Still, there are two chief pieces of evidence that those who view the United States as a rival predominate within Chinese security debates. First, China has pursued the greatest peacetime military buildup since the end of the Cold War and now has military capabilities that threaten the United States. Second, China pushes for Asian political forums that diminish U.S. influence. Beijing's treatment of domestic minorities provides further evidence that China is not the responsible power so many hoped it would be.

It is possible that in the coming years and decades, internal problems may cause a shift in China's external behavior. The PRC's domestic problems are real and numerous and cannot be fixed on the cheap. From reforming the broken pension system to addressing minority grievances properly, these domestic issues will require significant funds and extensive attention. Domestic problems and an economic slowdown may force China to focus more on solving internal problems, perhaps even taking seriously the calls for political reform coming from within China. On the other hand, the PLA and the internal security services are the CCP's final firebreak. It would be unwise for China's leaders to starve the PLA of resources.

While Chinese leaders view the United States as a rival and behave accordingly, should politics within China change, so may this perception of U.S. intentions. A government in China less afraid that others are trying to bring it down would act with less suspicion and prickliness abroad. But as long as the CCP fears many elements of its own society as well as the supposed acts of "foreign forces" to destroy it, it will continue to defend itself against these perceived threats. There is little the United States can do to change these perceptions; they are inherent in the way China organizes its politics. Ultimately, the future of Sino-American relations depends on how politics unfolds in Beijing.

Notes

1. See David Shambaugh, *China's Communist Party: Atrophy and Adaptation* (Berkeley: University of California Press, 2009).

2. Lampton, *The Three Faces of Chinese Power*, 61–66. See also Joshua Kurlantzick, *Charm Offensive: How China's Soft Power Is Transforming the World* (New Haven: Yale University Press, 2008).

3. "China's Defense Budget," Global Security, http://www.globalsecurity.org/military/world/china/budget.htm (accessed February 6, 2012).

4. Sean Chen and John Feffer, "China's Military Spending: Soft Rise or Hard Threat?" *Asian Perspective* 33, no. 4 (2009): 47–67.

5. David Shambaugh, "China's Military Making Steady and Surprising Progress," in *Strategic Asia 2005–2006*, ed. Ashley J. Tellis and Michael Wills (Seattle & Washington, D.C.: National Bureau of Research, 2005), 69.

6. David Lai, "Chinese Military Going Global," *China Security* 13 (2009), http://www.chinasecurity.us/index.php?option=com_content&view=article&id=221&Itemid=8#lai6.

7. See Lampton, *The Three Faces of Chinese Power*.

8. "Dujia diaocha: Zhongguoren renhe kan zhong mei guanxi?" [Exclusive investigation: How do Chinese view China-U.S. relations?], *Huanqiu Shibao* [*Global Times*], March 2, 2005, www.sohu.com. See also "Wu da chengshi minyi diaocha 56.7% renwei mei zai ezhi zhongguo" [Public opinion in five big cities shows 56.7% believe the United States is containing China], *Huanqiu Shibao*, March 2, 2005, www.ynet.com/view.jsp?oid=4774610&pageno=1.

9. Mark Leonard, *What Does China Think?* (New York: PublicAffairs, 2008), 104.

10. Information Office of the State Council of the People's Republic of China, "China's National Defense in 2006," December 2006, http://english.people.com.cn/whitepaper/defense2006/defense2006.html.

11. For more on incidents in the East China Sea, see Mark J. Valencia, "The East China Sea Dispute: Context, Claims, Issues, and Possible Solutions," *Asian Perspective* 31, no. 1 (2007): 127–67.

12. "China's National Defense in 2006;" Office of the Secretary of Defense, United States Department of Defense, *Military Power of the People's Republic of China 2008*, http://www.defenselink.mil/pubs/pdfs/China_Military_Report_08.pdf.

13. "China Planning to Secure North Korea's Nuclear Arsenal," *Agence France Press*, January 8, 2008, http://afp.google.com/article/ALeqM5iAEayq_x7zjS3Mz2eGruMU2QpQkQ.

14. According to the Stockholm International Peace Institute, Japan's defense budget as a percentage of GDP has stayed relatively constant at 1 percent between 1988 and 2010, http://milexdata.sipri.org/result.php4 (accessed July 7, 2011).

15. The defense expenditure of EU countries decreased in real terms by 1.4 percent in 2007, 3.8 percent in 2008, and 4.9 percent in 2009, http://www.eda.europa.eu/DefenceData (accessed July 7, 2011).

16. For more on PLA's ambivalent and often suspecting attitude toward the United States and its allies, see David Shambaugh, "China's Military Views the World: Ambivalent Security," *International Security* 24, no. 3 (1999/2000): 52–79.

17. Roger Cliff, Mark Burles, Michael S. Chase, Derek Eaton, and Kevin L. Pollpeter, *Entering the Dragon's Lair: Chinese Antiaccess Strategies and Their Implications for the United States* (Santa Monica, CA: RAND, 2007).

18. "More Than 1,400 Chinese Missiles Targeting Taiwan," *Kyodo News*, October 21, 2010, http://www.breitbart.com/article.php?id=D9J00IJO0&show_article=1; "China May Boost Missiles Aimed at Taiwan to 1,900," *Agence France Press*, July 22, 2010, http://www.defensenews.com/article/20100721/DEFSECT01/7210304/China-May-Boost-Missiles-Aimed-Taiwan-1-900.

19. The International Institute for Strategic Studies, "China: Air Force," in *The Military Balance 2000–2001* (Oxford: Oxford University Press, 2000), 197; The International Institute for Strategic Studies, "China: Air Force," in *The Military Balance 2011* (London: Routledge, 2011), 231.

20. Yitzhak Shicor, "The U.S. Factor in Israel's Military Relations with China," *China Brief* 5, no. 12 (2005), http://www.jamestown.org/single/?no_cache=1&tx_ttnews[tt_news]=3864.

21. Ronald O'Rourke, "China Naval Modernization: Implications for U.S. Navy Capabilities—Background and Issues for Congress" (Washington, D.C.: Congressional Research Service, 2011), 22.

22. Ibid., 43.

23. Ibid., 33.

24. Ibid., 42.

25. Office of the Secretary of Defense, U.S. Department of Defense, *Annual Report to Congress: Military and Security Developments Involving the People's Republic of China 2010*, http://www.defense.gov/pubs/pdfs/2010_cmpr_final.pdf, 33.

26. This belief demonstrates the continued influence of Mao's strategic thought in PLA thinking. See Mao Zedong, *On Protracted War* (Peking, China: Foreign Language Press, 1960).

27. Ashley J. Tellis, "China's Military Space Strategy," *Survival* 49, no, 3 (2007): 41–2.

28. Wang Hucheng quoted in Ibid., 49.

29. Ibid., 49.

30. Shane Harris, "China's Cyber-Militia," *National Journal*, May 31, 2008.

31. Rory Medcalf and Raoul Heinrichs with Justin Jones, *Crisis and Confidence: Major Powers and Maritime Security in Indo-Pacific Asia* (Double Bay, New South Wales, Australia: Lowy Institute for International Policy, 2011), http://www.lowyinstitute.org/publications/crisis-and-confidence-major-powers-and-maritime-security-indo-pacific-asia, 6.

32. See the following articles: David Lague, "Firepower Bristles in South China Sea as Rivalries Harden," Reuters UK, June 11, 2012; Max Boot, "China Starts to

Claim the Seas," *Wall Street Journal*, June 24, 2012; "Philippines: Chinese Boats Leave Disputed Lagoon," CBS News, June 26, 2012.

33. See Valencia, "The East China Sea Dispute."

34. "Japan and China Face Off over Energy," *Asia Times*, July 2, 2005.

35. Robert Sutter, "The PLA, Japan's Defense Posture, and the Outlook for China-Japan Relations," in *Shaping China's Security Environment: The Role of the People's Liberation Army*, ed. Andrew Scobell and Larry M. Wortzel (Carlisle, PA: Strategic Studies Institute, 2006), 182.

36. Shinji Hyodo, "First Ever Sino-Russian Joint Military Exercises: Russia Rapidly Moving Closer to China," *National Institute for Defense Studies News*, September 2005, http://www.nids.go.jp/english/publication/briefing/pdf/2006/092.pdf. More recently, in April 2012, China and Russia conducted their largest naval exercises in history.

37. Xie Zhijun, "Asian Seas in the 21st Century: With So Many Rival Navies, How Will China Manage?" *Junshi Wenzhai* (February 1, 2001): 20–22, quoted in Toshi Yoshihara and James Holmes, "The Influence of Mahan upon China's Maritime Strategy," *Comparative Strategy* 24, no. 1 (2005): 26.

38. Jiang Shiliang, "The Command of Communications," *Zhongguo Junshi Kexue* (October 2002): 106–114, FBIS-CPP20030107000189, quoted in James Holmes and Toshi Yoshihara, "China and the Commons: Angell or Mahan?" *World Affairs* 168, no. 4 (Spring 2006): 177.

39. Zhang Wenmu, "China's Energy Security and Policy Choices," *Shijie Jingji Yu Zhengzhi* 5 (May 14, 2003): 11–16, quoted in Holmes and Yoshihara, "China and the Commons."

40. Erica S. Downs, statement to the United States–China Economic and Security Review Commission, August 4, 2006, http://www.uscc.gov/hearings/2006hearings/written_testimonies/06_08_3_4wrts/06_08_3_4_dowes_erica_statement.pdf.

41. Hu Jintao allegedly urged a closed-door government session in 2003 to find ways around the "Malacca dilemma," namely the fact that much of China's seaborne trade, including oil, goes through the Malacca Strait. "Some major powers," he is reported to have said, were trying to assert control in the strait. Shi Hongtao, "Nengyuan anquan zaoyu 'Maliuya kunju' ZhongRiHan nengfou xie shou" [Energy security runs up against the 'Malacca Dilemma'; Will China, Japan, and Korea cooperate?], *Zhongguo qingnian bao* [*China Youth Daily*], June 15, 2004, business.sohu.com/2004/06/15/49/article220534904.shtml.

42. Ong, *China's Security Interests*, 126.

43. See James Holmes and Toshi Yoshihara, *Red Star over the Pacific: China's Rise and Challenge to U.S. Maritime Strategy* (Annapolis, MD: Naval Institute Press, 2010). Holmes and Yoshihara draw on a plethora of Chinese language documents written by Chinese strategists to support their claims regarding China's ambitions at sea.

44. Lampton, *Same Bed, Different Dreams*, 52–53.

45. U.S. Department of Defense, *The Quadrennial Defense Review*, 2006, 29.

46. Ibid., 29–30.

47. Ibid., 30.

48. U.S. Department of Defense, *The National Defense Strategy of the United States of America*, March 2005.

49. "SCO Wants Date for U.S. Withdrawal from Central Asia," *Daily Times*, July 6, 2005, http://www.dailytimes.com.pk/default.asp?page=story.

50. Speech of the Secretary-General of the Shanghai Cooperation Organization Bolat Nurgaliev at the Special Conference on Afghanistan, March 27, 2009; http://www.sectsco.org/EN/show.asp?id=55.

51. Stephen Blank, "China and the Shanghai Cooperation Organization at Five," Jamestown Brief, Volume 6, Issue 33 (May 9, 2007).

52. Chu Shulong, "China, Asia, and Issues of Sovereignty and Intervention," *Pugwash Occasional Papers* 2, no. 1 (2001), http://www.irchina.org/en/xueren/china/view.asp?id=808.

53. Here I use the standard definition of empire: a state that extends dominion over populations distinct culturally and ethnically from the culture and ethnicity at the center of power, as opposed to the more common contemporary form of government, a federation. In a federation, a large or small multiethnic state—or even an ethnically homogeneous one—relies on mutual agreement among its component political units, which retain a high degree of autonomy.

54. Ross Terrill, *The New Chinese Empire and What It Means for the United States* (New York: Basic Books, 2004), 3; "Does China Awake?," *Economist*, October 2, 2003.

55. Suisheng Zhao, "A State-led Nationalism: The Patriotic Education Campaign in Post-Tiananmen China," *Communist and Post-Communist Studies* 31, no. 3 (1998): 287–302.

56. Howard W. French, "Intellectuals in China Condemn Crackdown," *New York Times*, March 24, 2008.

57. Gang Lin, "China's Restless Minorities: Chinese Policy in Tibet and Xinjiang," Woodrow Wilson Center for Scholars, October 18, 2000, http://www.wilsoncenter.org/index.cfm?fuseaction=events.event_summary&event_id=3775.

58. "Trashing the Beijing Road—A Week in Tibet," *The Economist*, March 22, 2008.

59. Ibid.

60. "China: Tibetan Monasteries Placed Under Direct Rule," Human Rights Watch, (March 16, 2012), http://www.hrw.org/news/2012/03/16/china-tibetan-monasteries-placed-under-direct-rule.

61. Gardner Bovingdon, "The Not-So-Silent Majority: Uyghur Resistance to Han Rule in Xinjiang," *Modern China* 28, no. 1 (2002): 58.

62. "Under the Thumb; China's Far West," *Economist*, December 3, 2005.

63. Terrill, *The New Chinese Empire*, 236.

64. Lampton, *Three Faces of Chinese Power*, 68–77.

65. Tania Branigan, "China Launches Major Push to Invest in North Korea," *Guardian*, September 26, 2010, http://www.guardian.co.uk/world/2010/sep/26/china-push-invest-in-north-korea.

3

The U.S.-China Relationship: An Economist's Assessment

Phillip Swagel

Even while China is viewed as "Bad China" and a rival in the security sphere, the predominant view of China is that of "Good China" and a key trading partner. At least for now, in both countries the U.S.-China relationship is viewed as fundamentally "win-win" in the economic sphere. From the U.S. perspective, this is not for lack of recognition of the strategic challenges presented by China or for want of problems in the economic relationship, but rather because of the immense benefits resulting from trade and financial ties between the two nations. The consequences of a conflict—at any temperature—that leads to a serious diminution of the economic benefits from the U.S.-China relationship would mean slower growth, less job creation, and lower standards of living in both countries. This reality keeps the two nations together as partners, at least for now.

The dominance of the Good China point of view in U.S. policymaking reflects as well the judgment by policymakers that, while Chinese economic policy choices are not always what the United States would want (and not even always in China's own best interest), on the whole China makes a positive contribution to global growth and economic stability rather than the reverse. This is not the case in every instance by far: China certainly does not respect every principle of the international trading system (for example, it allows massive theft of intellectual property) and its imprudent monetary policy jeopardizes international financial stability by contributing to the formation of asset bubbles in China and abroad. But as an export economy dependent on a benign external environment and healthy foreign markets, China has generally avoided actions that would undermine global economic stability. During the Asian financial crisis of the late 1990s and the more recent global financial crisis, China took overt and costly steps to ensure global financial stability and to boost its own and global growth.

For the United States, the economic relationship with China boosts consumption and investment while helping to keep a lid on inflationary pressures. Tapping China as a platform for production and as a source of low-cost imports means an increased standard of living for the United States as a whole. In crass shorthand, U.S. families of all income levels enjoy more and better clothes, toys, televisions, and everything else now made in China (which sometimes feels like everything). Competitive pressure is uncomfortable for U.S. firms exposed to imports, but this impact of globalization boosts productivity and thus leads to higher overall U.S. wages and incomes. On the whole, the availability of imports from China contributes to a more prosperous United States, at least in the aggregate. This is the case even though some people find their wages under pressure from competition from China or their jobs moved overseas.

As is unfortunately typical with international trade, the benefits arising from the U.S.-China economic relationship are not evenly shared within the United States. Workers with relatively low skills face the most competition from Chinese imports and thus experience the most disruption; U.S. wages rise overall, but the gains are skewed to those with relatively high skills who can leverage the participation of China in the global economic system. In principle, it should be possible to spread the overall gains to those most adversely affected, but U.S. policies have not been effective at fostering gains-sharing or facilitating adjustment.

On the financial side, Chinese currency intervention to maintain an undervalued renminbi is effectuated by purchases of dollar assets such as Treasury bonds. This means that U.S. interest rates are lower than if the United States did not have access to global capital flows. China's determination to slow the appreciation of its currency helps to fund spending by U.S. families, firms, and the government (the latter through massive purchases of U.S. government securities). Lower interest rates mean a lesser cost to support a given level of spending, but they also provide an incentive for more spending by both government and the private sector—

a temptation, one might say, that the United States has not resisted. The downside of this lies in the accumulation of debt by U.S. households and the government and thus the potential for a period of slower consumption growth as these obligations are repaid and the corresponding resources are not available for use in the United States.

The fact that the mix of policies in China affects the United States and other nations imparts a responsibility on China for its actions to foster global financial stability. But Beijing has not always acted responsibly. Most critically, China's overly loose monetary policy over the past several years contributed to the credit bubble that gave rise to the financial crisis. While the crisis was not China's fault—after all, no one in China forced U.S. financial institutions to make risky loans or U.S. families to accept them—Chinese policies contributed to the low interest rates associated with lax lending standards. China's important role in the world economy necessitates a responsibility that remains to be fulfilled.

From China's perspective, commerce with the United States and other advanced economies has provided an avenue for rapid economic and technological advancement. China's output in 2006 was about thirteen times greater than in 1978,[1] and hundreds of millions of people have moved out of poverty. These achievements were made possible by the export engine harnessed to economic integration with the United States and other advanced economies. It is no small irony that the *successful* great leap forward of modern Chinese history came through a close relationship with capitalism and the Western world.

Through the Good China prism, continued growth in China is advantageous for both countries—the relationship is positive-sum now and will remain so into the future. Moreover, the economic view assumes that continued engagement with China will translate into future political and social liberalization. This comes about both because economic progress would stall without such liberalization, as Chinese growth increasingly depends on activities that depend on the free flow of information, and because the Chinese people will come to expect increased liberty to accompany material advancement. If this future is borne out, it will mitigate concerns over the conduct and intentions of a rising China. A China that is more liberal and democratic (in the classical sense) will become less of a threat to other countries.

The policy implications of the economic view tend strongly toward cooperation. China responds to positive incentives, under this view, because continued economic growth is vital for sustaining social harmony in China, and at least some degree of political and social liberalization is needed to maintain economic growth. This presents the CCP with a dilemma: its political legitimacy depends on continued economic growth and job creation, but to make this growth possible it must allow political liberalization that could undermine its preeminent role in Chinese society over time.

Optimists therefore assume that China will successfully traverse a path in which the Communist Party *very* gradually allows for an increased measure of political freedom and slowly puts its political dominance at risk. The alternative is that Chinese authorities, whether civilian or military, take steps to subvert increased freedom. This might bolster the status quo for a period, but it will also short-circuit growth and, over time, lead to a more rapid decline in the CCP's role. Growth and job creation should provide the key incentives for responsible behavior by Chinese authorities in the near term and to a more open and democratic Chinese society and political system over time.

There is some evidence that economic progress has affected social and political behavior. Advances in technology and communications, for example, have made it easier for public sentiment to form within China over issues such as working conditions, rising prices, and misbehavior by local political leaders, and on occasion have required national and local authorities to respond (examples include groundswells of popular anger over train crashes and criminal behavior by local officials and their relatives). At the same time, the supremacy of the CCP remains unchallenged. Moreover, technological and communications advances provide new means for the party to buttress its own position by rallying nationalist fervor against foreigners and outside influences. The key assumption of the Good China school—that material gains will bring about future changes in other dimensions—remains a hope rather than a necessary conclusion.

In considering the differences between the economic and strategic perspectives, it is vital to keep in mind differing time horizons, since the balance of interests will evolve and it is not necessarily the case that the economic viewpoint will prevail forever. The harmonious outcome envisioned in the economic perspective depends on the future direction of economic and political policies within China. It could be that China moves away from the role of a constructive participant in the international system and puts in motion a corresponding shift in the U.S.-China relationship. Three possible scenarios are explored in detail in the following chapter, including one that ends with a rupture in the bilateral relationship. Given the enormous economic cost this rupture would entail, it is hard to imagine that the Chinese authorities would look to make it happen. But this worst-case scenario could still take place, even if it is most likely to come about through policy mistakes in China rather than intentional measures.

For now, at least, China and the United States have important reasons to maintain an economic relationship from which both benefit tremendously. Recognizing this, even while acting as rivals along security dimensions, both countries mainly cooperate in economic and financial matters. Instances in which the two nations disagree, such as with certain trade disputes and on the currency issue, are notable for their self-contained character. Disputes occur, motivated by both domestic politics and substantive disagreements, but the underlying flows of trade and capital at the foundation of the relationship continue.

Broad U.S. Economic Interests with China

For the United States, the near-term benefits of the economic relationship with China are as a low-cost source from which to import both goods and capital.[2] The benefits of imports come about through greater variety and lower prices for traded goods, which translate into increased purchasing power for U.S. families across the income spectrum. The competition from Chinese companies, moreover, leads to higher productivity for U.S. firms.

One way of gauging the benefits of imports is to assess the gains to families from lower prices of goods they purchase for consumption. Furman (2005) finds that the benefits of lower prices for food resulting from the spread of so-called big-box retailers such as Wal-Mart was equivalent to an average of $782 per American family in 2003. For a broader range of products than just food, the gains came to $2,329 per household in 2004.[3] The largest percentage gains were for lower-income families, whose purchasing power was extended the most as a share of income as a result of lower prices. Some of these gains reflect improved technologies and better logistics within the retailing sector, but part of the gain reflects the lower import prices for which trade in competition is a key driver.

Low-priced imports further put competitive pressure on domestic firms, leading yet again to lower prices and increased purchasing power for American families. In the near term, competitive pressure from imports is uncomfortable for firms and workers in affected industries. Over time, however, this leads to productivity improvements as firms adapt to competitive pressure, and increased productivity in turn leads to higher wages and incomes, growth, and job creation.[4] Evidence that import competition fosters higher productivity can be seen in studies of individual industries and of economies as a whole. In the cement industry, for example, Dunne, Klimek, and Schmitz (2009) find that increased import competition led to changes in management practices that boosted productivity.[5] Looking across many industries in Europe, Bloom, Draca, and Van Reenen (2011) find that import competition from China boosted research and development, patenting activity, and productivity within firms while leading to a shift in industry employment toward more innovative and advanced firms.[6] On the other hand, Autor, Dorn, and Hanson (2011) find that import competition from Chinese products has negative impacts on local labor markets that offset one-third to two-thirds of the U.S. gains from trade with China.[7]

Capital inflows from China likewise have overall positive near-term impacts on the United States by reducing the cost of capital and boosting domestic investment. As discussed by Bernanke (2005), increased saving in emerging-market countries affects the United States through impacts on interest rates, the exchange value of the dollar, and equity and real estate prices.[8] In Bernanke's view, a global glut of saving has contributed to the U.S. current account deficit by pushing down yields and providing Americans with incentives for increased consumption.[9] Chinese purchases of dollar assets thus have a positive impact on the United States in the near term, since lower interest rates are generally associated with increased consumption, investment, and growth.

For the United States, low-cost imports and easy access to financing can both be connected to Chinese exchange rate intervention because maintaining an undervalued currency requires China to create reserves (electronic money) with which to buy dollars. The decision to maintain an artificially weak Chinese currency thus promotes both cheap imports and low-rate borrowing for the United States.

Estimates of the degree to which the renminbi is undervalued vary but are generally within the range of 10 to 30 percent.[10] The continued accumulation of foreign currency reserves, at just over $3 trillion at the end of 2011, is the embodiment of the policy intervention through which the Chinese government maintains the undervalued nominal exchange rate.

The weak renminbi boosts Chinese exports and indirectly underwrites American spending, but it is not cost free—indeed, there are substantial downsides for both China and the United States that become apparent with a longer horizon. From the U.S. perspective, China's actions help make the U.S. financial system fragile, and the U.S. economy vulnerable to disruptions. This was evident during the financial crisis and could become acute in the future, since cheap credit now would mean problems later if foreign financing dries up. This could lead to a spike in U.S. interest rates and a sharp retrenchment in investment and growth.

Even without such a crisis, ongoing capital inflows to finance the current U.S. account deficit generally mean ever-increasing foreign ownership of U.S. assets and the necessity of an ever-larger eventual future adjustment in which a greater share of U.S. income is devoted to paying foreign obligations. The longer the United States borrows from China and other countries, the greater will be the required increase in national saving to fund these repayments, and thus the more substantial the reduction in future U.S. consumption and investment. This could lead to difficult and painful adjustments, as American consumers and businesses accustomed to easy credit are forced to change their spending habits.

For China, the near-term dangers include inflation as a side effect of the money creation needed to maintain the exchange rate peg, along with possible financial sector problems from the combination of easy money and lax underwriting—a reprise of sorts of the crisis in the United States. A longer-term issue for China is that countries such as the United States that now run balance-of-payments deficits and absorb international capital flows will turn into savers, and this could make it difficult for China to sustain the export growth and job creation at a scale sufficient to maintain social harmony. China must shift toward growth driven by domestic spending to generate the jobs needed to absorb the continued influx of immigrants from rural areas and thereby avoid social unrest.

China has begun to make the transition to a new economic model, including finally starting an ongoing currency appreciation that will nudge production toward domestic Chinese consumers rather than U.S.–bound container ships. China has also begun to establish the infrastructure for the currency to be used in global transactions—a necessary precursor to moving toward a floating exchange rate. China announced in February 2011 that it would allow trading of yuan-denominated foreign-exchange options; this provides companies with financial instruments with which to hedge their exposure to currency changes. (Such hedging capability would not be needed in a regime with a fixed exchange rate.) In addition, foreign firms are now allowed to borrow in Chinese currencies through bond sales in Hong Kong and hold some renminbi deposits overseas rather than surrendering them to the Chinese government, and some trade between China and other Asian countries is now denominated in renminbi rather than dollars. While these steps will have only a modest impact in increasing the use of renminbi in global transactions, their greater importance is that they will lead financial institutions and companies in China and other countries to develop additional infrastructure to deal with renminbi-dollar transactions. They are an indication that China is moving toward allowing capital flows and a floating exchange rate.

These moves are timely. Chinese currency intervention contributes to inflationary pressures and mounting financial sector imbalances within China because avoiding the full currency appreciation requires China in effect to print money with which to buy dollar assets and thus to weaken the yuan. China is then forced to take further steps to keep the resulting bank reserves (money in electronic form) from leaking into the economy and thereby boosting inflation by bidding up asset prices. These steps are only partly successful, as overall inflation reached 6.5 percent in July 2011 but then fell under 4 percent in 2012 as the Chinese economy slowed. Similarly, press reports indicate that easy lending has spurred real estate price booms across China. If these turn into collapsing bubbles, the embedded losses would exact a huge price on the financial system.

China has taken a variety of measures to absorb the excess liquidity and head off inflation, including raising domestic interest rates, imposing higher reserve requirements on banks so they must hold onto cash rather than lend it out, and providing administrative guidance for banks to reduce risky lending. These steps are all aimed at reducing inflationary pressures and ensuring that the buildup of liquidity within China does not undermine the stability of the Chinese banking system.

The ad hoc nature of these banking and monetary policy actions only serves to highlight the benefits for China of phasing out its currency intervention. A faster currency appreciation would tamp down inflation without the distortions imposed by blunt actions such as administrative limits on bank lending. The stronger yuan would slow inflation directly through lower import prices and indirectly through increased competitive pressure on domestic Chinese firms. It would further reduce inflationary pressures through financial markets, since China would no longer need to buy dollars, and this would remove the impetus for excess credit growth and upward pressure on asset prices.

The modest pace of the currency appreciation to date appears to reflect concerns in China about the impact of slower export growth and thus weaker job creation. This hesitancy is natural, as exports were a key driver of net employment growth in China at least through 2005, according to Feenstra and Hong (2009).[11] The problem is that delay means increased inflationary pressures within China and wider imbalances in the international economy between saver nations such as China and borrower ones such as the United States. The costs of the continued currency peg are thus imposed not just on China, but also on other nations.

China faces substantial economic challenges even once monetary and currency policies are addressed. Many state-owned enterprises enjoy privileged access to credit from banks affiliated with various parts of the government, whether national, regional, or local. These affiliations give rise to poor lending decisions and loose credit conditions above and beyond those associated with the weak currency. Firms that have access to easy credit tend to have low productivity and thus soak up resources—financial, material, and personnel—that would be more productively deployed in other activities. Loosening the web of connections among firms, banks, and the government would likely lead to a better allocation of resources and thus higher productivity and stronger growth and job creation.

Responsible Versus Irresponsible Chinese Behavior

Chinese policy includes a mix of responsible and irresponsible behavior. China's imprudent exchange rate and monetary policy, for example, contribute to macroeconomic imbalances in both China and the United States, but at the same time China has avoided a harmful reversal of global financial flows and a massive sell-off of dollar assets. Similarly, China flouts parts of the global trading system, such as the protection of intellectual property rights, but worked to avoid a harmful trade war during the financial crisis and is a key U.S. trade partner.

An overall evaluation is thus complicated. There is huge room for improvement; on the whole, China's actions contribute to global growth and stability and foster an economic environment that benefits China, the United States, and other nations. There are real examples of how China's integration into the global financial system leads it to take certain responsible policy actions. Chinese policy does not result from some charitable attitude toward the United States but reflects China's own self-interest.

For China, the benefits from maintaining a harmonious economic relationship with the United States are immense; indeed, this relationship has been at the heart of China's development since the 1980s as the United States has provided a ready market for exports and a source for technological and managerial expertise. With relatively weak growth in other major export destinations such as Japan and Europe, there was no potential replacement market for Chinese exports (though in the future, it could be that other emerging nations become more important Chinese export markets than the United States). The willingness and ability of the United States to absorb rising Chinese output has been the key to the two nations' mutually beneficial, albeit bumpy, relationship.

In principle, Chinese surpluses could have been invested in countries other than the United States; eventually, however, the capital would flow through the United States, so the overall U.S. trade deficit is matched by an offsetting capital inflow even if not specifically with China. In the event, however, Chinese trade surpluses with the United States have been recycled directly into investments in (largely) U.S. Treasury securities and other securities effectively guaranteed by the U.S. government, such as bonds and mortgage-backed securities issued by Fannie Mae and Freddie Mac. This arrangement reflects the relative attractiveness of U.S. markets compared to other economies with less growth (Japan and Europe) or greater volatility (emerging markets other than China). The deal is straightforward: China accumulates wealth and stores it in a safe form, while the United States uses the funds to cover the gap between its spending and saving.

Massive Chinese trade surpluses have led Beijing to accumulate a bulging chest of dollar reserves.[12] These surpluses and the dollar stockpile reflect the constellation of Chinese and U.S. policies and economic realities: the still-undervalued renminbi; modest U.S. saving; and high savings rates in China driven by precautionary motives that reflect the weak social safety net and fraying familial bonds. Together this leads to an inflow of foreign capital into the United States and means that China and other foreign suppliers of these resources accumulate claims on the United States through the purchase of dollar assets such as Treasury securities.

The $3 trillion reserve buildup represents a tradeoff: China has sacrificed domestic consumption over the past decades in which the reserves have been accumulated but has the ability to use these resources in the future. This is subject, however, to changes in the value of the assets as China is exposed to the usual vicissitudes of the market. It is not clear, for example, that the decision to accumulate such a large stock of reserves was in China's best interest given the likelihood of substantial capital losses if the renminbi continues to strengthen against the dollar over time.[13] Such losses are probably a bygone conclusion as they were suffered when China overpaid for its Treasury holdings (where overpaying for a newly issued bond is equivalent to accepting too low an interest rate). The important policy issues going forward are how the reserves will be used and the extent to which the existence of the reserves creates a dynamic for constructive or unconstructive Chinese behavior. It could be the case, for example, that China acts constructively to foster a strong global and U.S. economy, since this will best maximize its return on dollar assets. Or instead, it could be that China seeks to use its financial holdings as leverage for other, non-economic, purposes.

Actions from either country that disrupt the economic benefits would change the calculus of costs and benefits and put the economic relationship at risk. China's aggressive stance in security matters has carried over to the economic sphere, including through actions such as cyber attacks on Google, other companies, and U.S. government agencies, and interference in exports of rare-earth minerals. Such irresponsible actions put the relationship at risk.

China's ongoing currency intervention is similarly disruptive in that it stokes political tensions while delaying needed global adjustments in which exporter nations such as China shift toward greater domestic demand, and importers such as the United States see increased exports and greater saving. The artificially weak renminbi helps sustain some Chinese exporters that would otherwise be uncompetitive, while raising the price of imported goods and services in Chinese markets. Reversing this and boosting Chinese consumption and imports would allow global growth to remain strong while bringing about a reduction in borrowing by debtor nations such as the United States. Chinese growth would be driven by consumption rather than trade and vice versa for the United States. Removing the Chinese policies that now hinder this rebalancing would help the United States avoid accumulating a debt burden that risks a crisis such as the sovereign problems faced by Greece, Ireland, and others in Europe.

Allowing for a faster currency appreciation would provide an incentive for resources within China to shift more rapidly from export- to domestic-oriented uses. This is happening to an extent through the combination of a slow appreciation of about 5 percent per year of the nominal yuan exchange value and higher inflation in China than in the United States, which adds another 3 to 5 percent shift in competitiveness against Chinese firms and toward those in the United States.[14] Adjustment is taking place but at a slow pace that could be sped up by allowing for more rapid nominal exchange rate appreciation. The immense benefits for China from the economic relationship with the United States in turn make the cost of irresponsible actions that put the relationship at risk equally immense. This does not mean that adventurism will not happen—witness the break-in attempts aimed at Google and other apparently state-sponsored cyberincidents aimed at the United States.

Even so, while China is a security rival of the United States, it is more typically a partner on economic issues. This includes broad partnership on both trade and financial issues, even though on both fronts there are substantial areas of tension. This duality is common in the U.S.-China relationship. Incidents such as that at Google reflect the blurring of lines between the economic and national security camps, as well as ongoing debates within China about the extent to which the relationship should remain cooperative rather than confrontational.

Irresponsible behavior in the economic sphere can be seen when a country acts without regard to the detrimental consequences its policies have on others or on the global system as a whole. This is distinct from a situation in which countries undertake actions in their own self-interest that disadvantage others. Crossing the line into outright irresponsibility would involve decisions that have little self-benefit and entail mainly harmful impacts on other states. Irresponsible behavior goes beyond instances where a country makes policy mistakes that mainly redound on itself—irresponsibility in the global sense involves not just poor judgment but also a spillover impact on others. China's continued lack of respect for intellectual property rights, for example, and its aggressive program of computer espionage fit into the category of irresponsible behavior since they have negative consequences for other countries and little benefit for China. There are, in fact, negative consequences for China because its spying and stealing of technology today invite incursions on its intellectual property in the future.

An indication of the policymaking struggle within China itself is that this sort of policymaking driven by long-term considerations is not always apparent in economic decision making, presumably because important policymakers are not fully comfortable with decisions that rely more on market mechanisms than on command-and-control. As with national security, economic policymaking can appear to be confused when it is being driven by a process of accommodation between different ideological or intellectual factions.

Some aspects of rivalry or incidents of irresponsible behavior in the economic relationship appear to reflect misjudgments and internal political pressures. This notably includes energy policy, where Chinese attempts to secure sources of oil raise global tensions while providing little additional energy security for China. Such folly can lead to conflict, and it remains important to understand the roots of Chinese actions and consider how the United States can shape Chinese behavior in ways that are mutually beneficial. Actions such as destabilizing commodity-oriented investments in Iran and Africa are distinct from the impact of growth in China on demand and prices for global commodities. The impact of China in boosting commodity prices is mainly organic in that it is a consequence of China's economic growth and not the result of some particular policy action.

Near-Term Shared Interests, Long-Term Rivalry?

The foundation of the more optimistic Good China school of thought is that countries act in their own self-interest subject to constraints and that China and the United States will continue to cooperate on this basis. Even while influential voices in China call for a more assertive foreign and defense policy, it remains unclear the end to which such aggressiveness would be aimed. What is China ambitious to achieve with its newfound power? An adventurous military or foreign policy that leads to a large-scale change in the U.S.-China economic relationship would severely reduce the strong Chinese growth that underpins political stability in China. It is hard to see any realistic gain from assertive policies offsetting these costs.

Adventurism is still possible: after all, China over the past several years has at times acted as if securing natural resources is in its best interests despite how this policy upsets other nations—even though China does not in fact gain economic security through exclusive access to resources (because China still faces the opportunity cost involved with higher world prices for any commodities it owns or controls).

This miscalculation on energy policy illustrates that China can make mistakes and fail to recognize when a cooperative approach is in its own

self-interest. Given the evident benefits to China of economic cooperation, it would be a huge miscalculation for China to subvert its relationship with the United States. The United States and other Chinese trading
partners have policy tools, such as limiting China's access to foreign markets, that could punish China. This would have costs for the United States
and other countries—the loss of the benefits of trade. But China's current
trade partners could obtain clothing, toys, and even electronics now
made in China from other emerging-market countries, even if at higher
prices (the cost of the sanctions could be measured as the higher price
paid to import from countries other than China). China would likely suf-
fer considerable difficulties from being shut out of global trade markets,
in large part because its economic system is so geared toward exports.
Chinese production would reorient toward domestic markets over time,
but there would be adjustment costs from an abrupt shift. Above all, this
sort of break would leave both countries bereft of the important economic
benefits that now hold the relationship together. This would be a huge
mistake by either country, at least if states act in the rational best interest
of their inhabitants.

China is far from an upstanding citizen of the international economic
system. Its economic misdeeds include wholesale theft of intellectual
property, spying and other malicious interference in electronic commerce,
misguided policies regarding natural resources discussed above, and an
inappropriate monetary policy and currency peg. Even with all of this and
more (not to mention loathsome behavior in the sphere of human rights),
China's overall response to the financial crisis suggests that it values and
understands its role in contributing to the stability of the global international system.

China did not buy especially large amounts of subprime mortgage-
backed securities that lost much of their value during the financial crisis,
but China was nonetheless intensely affected by the crisis. This is because
sharp economic slowdowns in trading partners such as the United States
during the events of fall 2008 turned into a slowdown for China, too.
Rather than retreating behind trade protectionism, China responded with
a domestic stimulus centered on public spending on infrastructure and
improvements to the social safety net. This was first and foremost aimed
at supporting China's own growth and job creation, and it appears to have

largely succeeded as Chinese income gains slowed but remained in high single digits. At the same time, China's stimulus had the positive effect of helping to buoy global growth at a time when there were few alternative sources of demand.

Perhaps even more telling is that China acted responsibly in turning aside Russian suggestions that the two countries sell dollar assets in a coordinated fashion in order to further financial market difficulties faced by the United States.[15] As the owner of a huge portfolio of dollar assets, China had an incentive to act responsibly to safeguard the value of these assets; it would have taken a massive capital loss from a dollar devaluation (and still could well take a gradual loss as the renminbi strengthens against the dollar going forward). Nonetheless, this responsible Chinese action deserves credit for helping to stabilize the world economy and avoid disruptions to global financial markets. China by far does not behave in this responsible fashion on every economic issue, but its actions during the financial crisis demonstrated a sense of responsibility and recognition of its place as a key stakeholder in the global economic order. China could do better and more, but it has demonstrated an awareness of its stake in the system and played a broadly constructive role in the global economy.

Continued responsible behavior would involve action along a variety of economic policy dimensions. These are actions that the United States would want to see but also would generally be desirable for China—the usual situation for a beneficial economic relationship. On the financial side, a continued gradual appreciation of the renminbi would have a number of beneficial impacts. These include helping to propel a change in the composition of the Chinese economy toward domestic production and increased consumption while increasing the competitiveness of U.S. exports and thus helping to rebalance U.S. growth toward higher saving and greater exports. At the same time, the effective tightening of monetary conditions associated with the revaluation of the renminbi would help to reduce excess liquidity in China and head off any further weakening of the Chinese financial sector (though a costly bank recapitalization using public funds might still be required).

Continued renminbi appreciation is desirable, but overly rapid appreciation might actually pose a problem for the United States, since an abrupt weakening of the dollar or pause in foreign purchases of dollar assets could lead to spikes in U.S. interest rates and impose a drag on the U.S. economy. The threat of low demand for "safe" Treasury securities seems distant while the U.S. economic recovery remained muted through the fall of 2011 and while financial woes in Europe make Treasury investments a safe harbor. But this will eventually become a concern as the rebound proceeds and if Europe rights itself. In its steps to ensure relative stability in financial flows, China is acting in its own self-interest, but what is striking is the degree to which this matches with U.S. interests. This is the key characteristic of the economic view of the bilateral relationship.

Other responsible policy steps by China would operate over the medium term, including continuing to safeguard and deepen the broadly open trade relations between the two countries. Responsible measures include avoiding new trade disputes and resolving existing ones through full implementation of Chinese commitments to open markets and to eschew market-distorting policies. Over time, U.S. exports to China could grow as rising incomes lead Chinese citizens to demand both higher-quality goods, for which U.S. manufacturers are more competitive, and especially services. Given China's strength in manufacturing, it is not clear that the United States will ever fully close the bilateral trade deficit with China, which has run at an annual rate of $200 to $300 billion in recent years. While the level of the trade balance with one country is of limited macroeconomic meaning, maintaining strong U.S. growth while boosting national saving will require increased exports.[16]

China could undertake a range of actions in line with a commitment to responsible participation in the global economic system. China would ensure financial sector stability, including by a public recapitalization of the banking sector as needed. Tangible actions to protect intellectual property rights would form the basis for a future regime aimed at protecting Chinese intellectual property; this balance will inevitably shift with the continued development of the Chinese economy.[17] Allowing for the increased independence of the judiciary in resolving commercial disputes would complement intellectual property protection to foster an improved investment climate and help sustain growth in both countries. While resolution of political disputes remains the province of CCP insiders rather than the people of China, serious issues will increasingly arise in the case of disputes involving enterprises connected with the government or party at some level. This conflict will present a choice for China in terms of its ability to abide by the norms of the international system.

Responsible economic behavior would also involve action in areas that connect with security policy, including playing a positive role in safeguarding existing global energy supplies and helping to resolve disputes with countries such as Iran and Sudan. Chinese behavior that at times obstructs resolution of these disputes indicates a lack of recognition that these issues have both economic and security dimensions—or, perhaps because both aspects are present, this leads to difficulties in the formation of policy within China. It will be helpful over time for Chinese policymakers to understand that the interconnected nature of the U.S.-China economic relationship means that any efforts by China to "hurt" the United States would likely have severe negative consequences for China as well.

Over the longer term, optimists see Chinese policy as inevitably moving toward an economy based on an increased role for domestic growth and an economy in which a more robust social safety net reduces the need for families to keep large savings as buffers against economic shocks.[18] These changes are likely to involve a shift to a service-based economy rather than one dominated by manufacturing, simply because rising incomes among Chinese families will result in increased demand for services. The exchange of services is inexorably wrapped up with the exchange of information, and this requires internal and external openness to ideas and information. A domestic-driven economy will involve increased imports, and this likewise will require increased freedom of movement of ideas along with goods.

Such changes are both necessary and inevitable because the present model of Chinese growth is unsustainable. China cannot continue to enjoy 10 percent growth based on exports:[19] there are not enough markets in the rest of the world to support this growth. Continuing the unsustainable Chinese growth model will impose instability as other countries eventually face difficulty repaying their borrowing. From a Chinese perspective, a continuation of export-driven development would be a bad idea in that it would mean slow consumption growth and excess saving in China, yet again postponing the rewards of Chinese modernization. This calculus is well understood in China. The difficulty is in making a smooth transition in which export growth remains strong enough to create jobs even while the domestic-oriented economy expands. Guo and N'Diaye find that this change in economic orientation will eventually lead to increased employment but with important near-term dislocations as less-skilled workers lose jobs with export-oriented manufacturers and must acquire new skills to be absorbed into service-sector positions.[20] This transition explains the hesitancy of action among Chinese policymakers.

Conclusion

The cooperative U.S.-China economic relationship and broadly responsible Chinese approach to economic policymaking will not necessarily last forever. As China continues to develop rapidly and eventually draws near to the U.S. standard of living, China could see alternative economic arrangements, including its own domination of Asia, as a suitable model. Or put differently, over time the cost of Chinese actions that change the relationship could diminish as China derives less benefit from the bilateral relationship with the United States. This long-term possibility is the essence of strategists' concerns, and it is a valid one. This makes it important to understand the concerns of strategists over the more mercantilist view of U.S.-China relations and the distinction between the positive-sum (or win-win) approach of economists and the zero-sum view of strategists.

Bridging the gap between the Good China and Bad China schools means recognizing that China is both rival (in the security sphere) and partner (in the economic sphere). This duality is unlikely to change in the next decade, and it inevitably means that tensions between economic and national security considerations will remain.

Underneath any tensions, however, is the reality that both countries benefit immensely from the economic relationship. American families' standards of living are higher as a result of access to global markets including China, and Chinese growth has been propelled by its access to export markets in advanced economies such as the United States. These benefits mean that there would be huge costs to actions that seriously upset the economic status quo. These costs will not deter all adventurism, and they do not remove the possibility of policy mistakes. But the costs of an outright rupture are immense and likely to deter such an event until the calculus changes.

Notes

1. Bergsten et al., "China's Challenge to the Global Economic Order," in *China's Rise*, 9.

2. The inflow of capital mirrors the trade deficit in goods and services, as the U.S. financial account surplus matches the current account deficit in magnitude. One way to think of this is that the trade deficit represents U.S. consumption and investment involving more resources than are available domestically and making up the shortfall by bringing in foreign resources. These capital inflows are paid for by selling assets; thus, foreigners receive claims on future U.S. income in exchange for current goods and services.

3. See Jason Furman, "Wal-Mart: A Progressive Success Story," Center for American Progress, November 28, 2005, http://www.americanprogress.org/kf/walmart_progressive.pdf.

4. This point is emphasized by Alan Greenspan, *The Age of Turbulence: Adventures in a New World* (New York: Penguin Press, 2007).

5. Timothy Dunne, Shawn Klimek, and James A. Schmitz, Jr., "Does Foreign Competition Spur Productivity? Evidence from Post–WWII U.S. Cement Manufacturing" (Research Department Staff Report, Federal Reserve Bank of Minneapolis, 2009), http://www.minneapolisfed.org/research/events/2009_05_01/dunne.pdf.

6. Nicholas Bloom, Mirko Draca, and John Van Reenen, "Trade Induced Technical Change? The Impact of Chinese Imports on Innovation, IT, and Productivity" (Working Paper 16717, National Bureau of Economic Research, 2011).

7. David H. Autor, David Dorn, and Gordon H. Hanson, "The China Syndrome: Local Labor Market Effects of Import Competition in the United States" (mimeo, Department of Economics, Massachusetts Institute of Technology, 2011), http://econ-www.mit.edu/files/6613.

8. Ben S. Bernanke, "The Global Saving Glut and the U.S. Current Account Deficit" (speech to the Virginia Association of Economists, Richmond, VA, March 10, 2005), www.federalreserve.gov/boarddocs/speeches/2005/200503102/.

9. Francis E. Warnock and Veronica Cacdac Warnock find that international capital flows reduced interest rates on ten-year Treasury bonds by ninety basis points in 2004–2005. See their "International Capital Flows and U.S. Interest Rates," *Journal of International Money and Finance* 28 (2009): 903–19.

10. Wayne M. Morrison and Marc Labonte, *China's Currency: An Analysis of the Economic Issues* (Washington, D.C.: Congressional Research Service, 2011), 11.

11. The authors find that rising domestic demand generated three times the employment of exports, but this was entirely offset by increased productivity in production aimed at the domestic market, leaving exports as a key driver of net job creation. See Robert C. Feenstra and Chang Hong, "China's Exports and Employment," in *China's Growing Role in World Trade*, ed. Robert C. Feenstra and Shang-Jin Wei (Chicago: University of Chicago Press, 2010), 167–201.

12. "Gold & Foreign Exchange Reserves," People's Bank of China, http://www.pbc.gov.cn/publish/html/2011s09.htm (accessed July 8, 2011).

13. On the other hand, Joshua Aizenman, Menzie Chinn, and Hiro Ito find that the configuration of monetary policy choices by Asian economies involved with the accumulation of reserves has provided macroeconomic benefits by helping to stabilize real exchange rate fluctuations. See their "Surfing the Waves of Globalization: Asia and Financial Globalization in the Context of the Trilemma," *Journal of the Japanese and International Economies* 25, no. 3 (2011): 290–320.

14. The sum of the nominal change in the value of the currency and the inflation differential is the change in the real exchange rate, which is a better measure of the overall change in competitive conditions between Chinese and foreign firms than the nominal exchange rate alone. This is because higher inflation in China than in the United States corresponds to a loss of competitiveness among Chinese firms that is not reflected in the nominal exchange rate alone. As discussed next, these effects are related in that the actions to maintain the currency peg boost inflation in China.

15. This incident is recounted by Henry M. Paulson Jr., *On the Brink: Inside the Race to Stop the Collapse of the Global Financial System*, (New York: Business Plus Publishing, 2010).

16. Martin Feldstein discusses the rule of exchange rate movements in spurring a reduction of U.S. and Chinese current account imbalances, with increased consumption in China and higher saving in the United States being driven in part by an appreciation of the renminbi. Feldstein sets out the real exchange rate calculations discussed above. See Martin Feldstein, "The Role of Currency Realignments in Eliminating the U.S. and China Current Account Imbalances" (speech at the American Economic Association annual meeting, Denver, CO, January 2011).

17. For a discussion of Chinese practices regarding intellectual property rights, see U.S. International Trade Commission Report No. 332–514, *China: Intellectual Property Infringement, Indigenous Innovation Policies, and Frameworks for Measuring the Effects on the U.S. Economy*, November 2010.

18. Marcos Chamon and Eswar Prasad find that the rising household saving in China is explained by a combination of increased private spending on housing, education, and health care, along with a precautionary motive reflecting the difficulty Chinese families face in borrowing and the low rates of return on saving. Rising expectations for living standards, including better housing, education, and health care, thus translate into increased saving to fund these

large, lumpy expenditures. See their "Why Are Saving Rates of Urban House-holds in China Rising?" (Working Paper 14546, National Bureau for Economic Research, 2008).

19. Kai Guo and Papa N'Diaye demonstrate that the scope for export-led growth is limited even if China succeeds in moving into increasingly high-valued and more advanced exports. See their "Is China's Export-Oriented Growth Sustainable?" (Working Paper WP/09/172, International Monetary Fund, 2009).

20. Ibid.

4

Potential Long-Term Outcomes: Three Scenarios for China's Future

Dan Blumenthal and Phillip Swagel

China is growing rapidly, but it still has serious long-term economic issues with which it must grapple. Its social safety net is inadequate, with uneven access to health care services for many citizens. Its pension systems lag behind the development of the Chinese economy, leaving many workers to self-fund retirement savings rather than having a mix of portable public and private benefits. China's financial system escaped the worst of the financial crisis related to subprime lending, but China faces a possible real estate bubble of its own. Low-quality lending such as directed credit to state-owned enterprises allows poorly performing firms to survive while diverting resources from the more dynamic private sector. Further bailouts of Chinese banks are likely; a wholesale reform of China's state-centric system of capitalism is needed. China's education system remains inadequate and poorly suited to a future in which the Chinese economy will continue to shift from manufacturing to services and from building things to inventing them. The weak regime for the protection of intellectual property will hinder Chinese growth in key areas such as technology. And environmental protections continue to lag, as reflected in continued challenges in the quality of air and water. This is a huge list of challenges facing China's leadership, and these challenges apply on a massive scale—the norm with China. Against these challenges, $3 trillion of reserves is more understandable as a fund for action.

China is likely to be consumed with dealing with these challenges for a considerable period into the future. At some point, however, China's growth (if it continues) will put the country in position to think more broadly—and possibly to contemplate a negative change in its relationship with the United States.

The differences between economic and security-oriented views of China depend on future outcomes for Chinese development that are intrinsically uncertain. China's rising economic power could be worrisome if it translates into military and strategic power that is then put to use in ways that specifically threaten the United States. The opposite case would have China's rising prosperity leading to greater political and social freedoms. This would be the case in which global economic integration leads to political and social integration and smoother relations. The extent to which China's growth and prosperity contributes to broader global harmony will depend on the uses to which these economic advancements are put.

While the future is not knowable, it is useful to consider several trajectories for Chinese development, both political and economic, and then relate these trajectories to issues of regional and global security. This will not necessarily bridge the gap between the Good China and Bad China schools, but it makes clear some of the key tradeoffs between economic progress and security concerns.

Three scenarios are presented below: optimistic, somewhat pessimistic, and very pessimistic. Having chosen these labels, it must be noted that even the optimistic case is not filled with starry-eyed optimism. At best, economic and security relations between the United States and China will remain subject to strains, threats, and misunderstandings. At worst, the relationship will veer toward outright rivalry in both the economic and security spheres. The challenge is to find a way forward and for the United States to influence China toward the mutually beneficial path of the optimistic outcome.

The scenarios discussed below include:

1. Optimistic: China becomes wealthier and gradually becomes less authoritarian and simultanously a more responsible participant in the international system.

2. Somewhat pessimistic: China becomes rich but stays authoritarian and increasingly challenges or even threatens the United States in both economic and security spheres.

3. Very pessimistic: China's economic growth derails, leading
   to a period of internal instability that contributes to severe
   global instability.

Of these scenarios, Good China adherents clearly see the optimistic
scenario as most likely, with the caveat that "gradually" is the key word;
a move away from a politically repressive regime could take decades,
and it is difficult to plan for an event at such a distant horizon. One
central difference between the two pessimistic scenarios is the degree
to which China intentionally butts heads with the United States in the
security arena.

In the first scenario, Chinese prosperity provides an incentive for
the CCP and the Chinese government to act to ensure global harmony.
In contrast, the second scenario envisions development leading to conflict. This could be the case, for example, with a China that assertively
converts its newly gained material progress into an outward-oriented
scheme to secure further economic advantage. (This discounts the
possibility that the CCP would actually seek to impose its political
dominion over a society removed from China's border.) The third
scenario is a darker vision in which economic problems lead to destabilizing security ruptures.

The United States must consider potential policy responses for all
three cases. If China moves in an aggressive direction in the context
of the third scenario, the options will not be pleasant—ultimately, this
could involve an arms race and a reversion to the pre-1990s situation
with the Soviet Union. One complication is that this adversary will be
much richer and more connected in economic terms to both the United
States and other countries than the first Communist threat. This gives
the United States potential policy levers with which to influence China's
trajectory and to affect Chinese behavior, but at a cost to the United
States of giving up benefits from the economic relationship. The first
and second scenarios are simpler for U.S. policy, mainly requiring the
United States to avoid mistakes and (hopefully) to take advantage of
opportunities for further progress as they arise.

Scenario 1: Optimistic

The first scenario is something between a benign and an optimistic outcome in which the bilateral economic relationship remains strong, while there is a gradual evolution within China toward political and social freedom. On the economic side, this scenario is anchored by China addressing its current economic challenges, including normalizing its monetary policy and gradually ending its currency intervention. As a result, the composition of Chinese growth shifts toward domestic demand, and the nation liberalizes trade and financial flows. The external environment remains benign as U.S. and world growth recovers after the collapse of world trade in the wake of the recent financial crisis. Chinese growth remains strong, but its composition gradually shifts from being export- and investment-led, and thus imbalanced and unsustainable, to a path driven more by domestic consumption. The key term here is *gradual*, with Chinese domestic demand picking up slowly, and export flows morphing into increased imports (though not increasing enough to result in an outright trade deficit).

Along the way, the CCP eases its remaining hold on the economy in the spheres of information, communications, capital flows, and internal migration. This moderation comes about not because of any intrinsic change of heart on the part of CCP leadership, but because greater freedom will be a necessary adjunct to long-term economic development as the economy turns gradually toward more knowledge-intensive activities that cannot prosper in the face of repression. In the best case (and thus least likely or imminent), political suppression gradually eases as well, although China will not become a multiparty democracy. Indeed, a fully democratic endpoint seems quixotic in the context of a scenario in which growth continues smoothly, since the transition to this would likely prove chaotic. An outcome along the lines of Singapore is perhaps the best that can be expected, with Chinese citizens enjoying considerable freedom in their personal affairs but circumscribed political liberty. While not conforming to precepts of a Western democracy, this would be a huge improvement from the situation of today both for the world as a whole and for the people of China. This may be what CCP leaders want, but given China's size it might be impossible to achieve.

The economic evolution involves a relaxation of restraints on access to the media, the Internet, and other sources of information as well as an end to the government's interference in the allocation of capital. Monetary and exchange rate policy is normalized, with an end to the overly weak renminbi coupled with a broad tightening of monetary policy. The renewal of renminbi appreciation, even at a slow pace, in mid-2010 is a hopeful sign in this regard. This change in the exchange rate by itself provides a market-based incentive for the reallocation of resources from the export sector to domestic-focused production and thus for a rebalancing of the economy. This transition presents a key source of danger in that it will be difficult for some (perhaps many) Chinese firms to survive without the artificial crutch of the weak renminbi. The transition to a domestic-oriented economy will thus involve a temporary period of slower job growth and possibly increased unemployment as firms reorient their production to supply new internal markets. The economic infrastructure of China might not be sufficient to support increased domestic spending. Chinese ports for export have world-class logistics, but the same is not necessarily the case for internal transport, and this is what will matter for growth to reorient inward.

These concerns should not lead China to pause before undertaking this necessary adjustment, however, because China has the ability to counteract the risks involved with the stronger currency and economic transition. It is a reasonable concern that a stronger renminbi will lead to weak growth and increased unemployment until the domestic market picks up enough to absorb the laid-off workers from the export sector. But China has a ready policy offset, which is to dip into its ample dollar reserves to fund a fiscal stimulus. This is exactly what China did with apparently good results in response to the collapse of global trade during the financial crisis. The transition from an export-oriented economy to one focused on domestic consumption will feel much like the external shock of the crisis. Firms will find themselves without demand for their products and be forced to adapt. By spending its foreign currency reserves in the form of infrastructure (capital both physical and human) and perhaps tax relief, the Chinese government will boost domestic consumption and investment and offset lagging exports. Allowing for a stronger renminbi will make China's economy permanently more resilient and less vulnerable to slow foreign growth. China will thus make a one-time use of its reserves for the permanent benefit of a more balanced and resilient economy.

A second danger is in the rot lying within the financial system, which does not allocate capital effectively. One legacy of low-quality lending is that a slowing of growth along the transition path to an inward-oriented economy will lead to financial problems such as bank failures.[1] The salve to this is again to use Chinese foreign currency reserves to recapitalize the Chinese banking system. This will run down Chinese official resources, but it is a necessary move to avoid a worse outcome from a financial sector panic. A revitalized financial sector could better serve China's growing economy. This requires a new financial regulatory regime that both protects against poor lending and shields banks from pressures to make loans to politically influential prospective borrowers.

In this optimistic scenario, controls on inflows of foreign capital are gradually lifted as well. This would ease inward investment by foreign firms and encourage technology transfers and innovation by domestic Chinese firms (some of which now compete with global leaders but many of which simply produce for them instead). Left standing would be restrictions on foreign investment along the lines of those in advanced economies, including limits on investment in certain sectors such as security, media, and transport. As China shows itself to be a responsible participant in the international economic system, it would be natural for other countries to become less hesitant at the prospect of Chinese acquisitions of their companies. This trust building, however, will take years, though the process could be accelerated by overt Chinese policy actions such as cracking down on intellectual piracy and on Internet hacking emanating from China.

With liberalization, China's horde of foreign currency reserves—its enormous accumulation of dollar assets such as Treasury securities— would be largely redundant. China would no longer seek to repress artificially the value of the renminbi by accumulating foreign currency because this would be counterproductive and risk inflationary problems. Once the economy is reoriented from exports and the remaining export sector is competitive without the crutch of currency manipulation, further reserve accumulation would squander valuable resources because this would involve investing in lower-yielding securities such as U.S. Treasury bonds rather than higher-payoff projects in China itself. The reserves left after paying for a financial sector bailout and after spending to support social stability during the transition away from the export-oriented economy would become a rainy-day fund for action in the event of a future business cycle downturn.

The outcome in this scenario would be a continuation of strong Chinese growth. There could be slowdowns as Chinese industries are shaken by the end of the export-driven growth process, but this would be balanced by new opportunities to service a rapidly growing domestic market. As discussed by Guo and N'Diaye, the long-term prospect after rebalancing is for higher employment not lower.[2]

From the Chinese perspective, this scenario seems fraught with danger. Its outcome, after all, involves enormous and possibly wrenching changes in an economic model that has "worked" for the past two decades. The challenge for Chinese policymakers is that the current growth path is unsustainable. Chinese growth is unbalanced, shaped by a legacy of overly loose monetary policy and poor supervision of financial services firms. Left unchanged, the resulting crisis will make the financial crisis of 2008 in the United States and other advanced economies look tame because the scale of Chinese bad-lending practices is so vast. The United States is likely to chalk up a 3 percent decline in output over the course of the postcrisis recession. But other currency crises, such as those in Argentina, Thailand, Russia, or Indonesia, have involved much deeper collapses of output, and this could be the outcome in China absent a change of course. Indeed, such an economic collapse is precisely the third scenario discussed below.

Achieving this optimistic scenario involves continuing with economic liberalization, but making wholesale changes in other aspects of China's economic strategy. China has shown the capacity to take large economic steps, including recently with its fairly successful response to the financial crisis. A domestic-focused stimulus in China appears to have succeeded in propping up demand while being consonant with the long-run goal of stronger domestic spending from the private sector.

The changes in China would be deep. One common feature is that these changes would be driven by economic necessity—the need to allow for the political liberalization that would allow for continued material gains. These changes would include:

- A more appropriate monetary and financial policy. The weak exchange rate and loose monetary policy lead to an inefficient concentration of output in the export-oriented sector and to the neglect of domestic consumption.

- Improving financial sector regulation and allowing for the full application of monetary policy tools to the financial sector, both in order to reduce the prospects for yet another future financial sector crisis after the one now built into the system is resolved.

- Tackling corruption and the inconsistent application of the rule of law.

- Development of a social safety net including health care and pension systems. These would boost private expenditure, as Chinese families are unlikely to spend in earnest absent a safety net to replace the eroding structure of the extended family unit.

- Relaxation of information flows, notably including the Internet. State controls on information-related sectors will become an increasing hindrance to growth, and it is this economic and financial pressure that is most likely to lead to political liberalization.

- Dealing with issues relating to poor governance, corruption, and the lack of transparency in the judicial system. This will become a matter of economic necessity, as the current system will hold back growth. It is unclear, though, whether greater freedom of information will translate into increased freedom and greater participation in the political process. This question is linked to the future role of the CCP.

- Reducing the role of industrial policy, with China no longer targeting or protecting industries beyond a "normal" amount done by advanced economies.

- Allowing for free(r) trade. Less-fettered trade will put greater competitive pressure on domestic firms and boost Chinese productivity growth and incomes. At the same time, some Chinese firms will come under pressure, and there would be a larger number of people hurt by import competition. This, in turn, would put stress on the social safety net.

- Allowing for increased fiscal federalism. More Chinese government functioning and spending are done at a local level than in most advanced economies. Pensions and health care, for example, are localized. This leads to inefficiently small-scale provision and failure to spread best practices, and hindered mobility because pensions and other benefits are not easily transferred across regions.

Changes to monetary and financial policy will be necessary above all else to sustain Chinese growth because these steps are needed to ensure an effective allocation of resources as China's economy continues to develop. Sustained growth will require China to allow market forces, rather than party dictates and political connections, to allocate capital. Allowing foreigners to invest more freely in China and for the Chinese to invest overseas would boost the efficiency of China's financial system by sheer dint of competitive forces: to stay in business, banks and their borrowers would be forced to make better use of China's prodigious saving since otherwise these would turn to foreign institutions instead.

A more efficient allocation of capital would boost productivity growth by ensuring that the most efficient firms have access to funding for investment. A more dynamic financial sector would also mean improved returns for Chinese savers and thus higher incomes. Higher incomes would, in turn, support increased consumption and spur the necessary shift in the composition of the Chinese economy. Liberalized capital markets will accelerate the changes in the Chinese economy necessary to ensure that growth does not falter. The reward is what economists call an income effect—increased flows of returns from the same amount of saving—meaning that Chinese families in this future scenario will be able to save less and spend more and thus raise the material welfare of Chinese families.

Under this scenario, continued Chinese growth provides further economic benefits to the United States as well as political and social benefits to China and the world. China grows and becomes a market for U.S. goods and services, develops innovations that boost global productivity, and improves the quality of life of Americans. This is in line with the postwar development of Western Europe and Asian countries such as Japan, Korea, and Taiwan.

This benign scenario has important security and foreign policy implications, notably a relaxation of current tensions. This does not mean that China forgoes a military buildup; indeed, the present weak (in Chinese eyes) PLA armed forces might be seen as a historical anomaly that will be redressed under any likely economic and political scenario. But with further economic growth and political liberalization, China will have an even deeper interest in and desire for harmonious global relations, so the focus of Chinese military efforts will evolve to promote international stability rather than project Chinese power.

In this scenario, China's conception of its military role would evolve in several practical ways. The Chinese military would increase transparency, of both its strategic intentions and its specific capabilities, in an effort to ease tensions in the region and boost the confidence of other nations in dealing with China. China would also adhere to long-accepted interpretations of international law regarding exclusive economic zones and rights of maritime access. This would serve twin purposes that increase regional stability. First, it would foster a common legal interpretation that would allow for smoother settlement of territorial disputes. Second, increasing confidence of the United States and neighbors could lead to China's playing a greater role in ensuring freedom of access in important sea lanes. China would also desist from taking destabilizing actions such as pointing over 1,000 missiles across the Taiwan Strait.

It is hard to envision China moving in the direction of Canada or Europe in spending less on security or having no tensions or competition with the United States. But the political and security relationship could evolve towards cooperation on addressing common threats such as piracy and terrorism. In fact, China has already engaged in humanitarian assistance/disaster relief missions ranging from antipiracy operations in the Gulf of Aden to reconstruction work in postearthquake Haiti in 2010. Continued and increased missions of this sort would build international goodwill, especially when carried out in cooperation with other militaries. In an optimistic scenario, these activities would serve as a paradigm for how the Chinese military would operate in the Asian region itself.

During a long transition, however, the United States would still devote substantial resources toward hedging against potential Chinese threats. Progress toward changed security perceptions in Washington and Beijing that leads to some security cooperation could take decades. Still, if it happens, it is most likely to be the result of the continued economic relationship spilling over into the strategic realm.

A China that shifts toward democratic capitalism would lift the financial repression facing individuals, enforce the rule of law, and retreat from a system of crony capitalism intertwined with industrial policy. In other words, China would develop the social prerequisites for democracy. The puzzle today is why China is not yet a democracy, given its rapidly advancing level of development. According to such scholars as Seymour Lipset and Henry Rowen, once a country achieves a certain level of per capita production, democracy is just around the corner as the middle class demands greater political participation.[3]

One answer to this puzzle is that China is not really capitalist. It may have more private ownership and considerably increased market activity than before the 1980s, but still lacks the underlying social structures and values that make a country capitalist. These societal values and structures include much greater degrees of social capital and social trust than exist today, especially since the traditional kinship networks that have served as both lubricant and cohesive force in Chinese society are breaking down as the result of the one child policy.[4] A transition of the kind described in this scenario is made all the more difficult because the CCP has not allowed the development of an independent civil society and institutions rooted in the rule of law that could enforce contracts and protect property and investments. If China turns truly *capitalist,* as this optimistic scenario envisages, there is a much greater chance that predictions made by the Good China school regarding democratic transitions could occur. But the road to this point would be fraught with dangers. The system of crony capitalism would be slowly demolished, meaning that many elites would lose their privileged place in society and possibly their fortunes. It would take a strong leadership to challenge the entrenched powers that make China's economic system run today.

Singapore might be an attractive model from the Chinese perspective, but it is sui generis—a city-state so small as to be analogous to no other country. China is so large that its fiscal federalism would have to be accompanied by political federalism to better manage the diverse array of interests that span the countryside. The key to reform in China would be to strengthen the system of law. In a low-trust society such as China, law is even more vital than in high-trust societies such as Japan or to some extent the United States, which, as Tocqueville observed, has high degrees of spontaneous association that encourage trust.[5] The low-trust problem will be compounded by the breakdown of large families, a result of the one child policy and therefore the breakdown of the old *guanxi* networks that made Chinese enterprises run. Again, institutions such as property rights, contract law, criminal prosecutions, and an open media that can take on corruption will be essential to a successful transition to real capitalism and then liberal democracy.

Sino-U.S. relations would greatly improve if the transition described in this scenario comes about. First, the trade imbalances that today cause friction would gradually dissipate. Second, China would turn into a more transparent and international law-abiding country, making the United States far more likely to trust China in areas beyond economics, including national security. Third, China would truly have a deep stake in the liberal international system and its manifold rules. The idea not only in the United States, but also throughout the West, that China distorts and disobeys the international rules to its own benefit would become far less salient. Fourth, if China moved in this direction, it would need to devote more time and attention to domestic concerns—the enforcement of law, the building of a social safety net, the struggles with elites who have a stake in the old system, and the problems of the rural population, including ethnic minorities. China would be far less likely to focus on a destabilizing military buildup and far more likely to attend to its economic and social problems.

A more liberal and capitalist China could encourage greater trust in the international security system. The United States would see a China becoming more free and perhaps even moving toward democratization. Chinese society would presumably face debates over the use of public resources—a real "guns versus butter" discussion—and more transparency in military affairs. Over time, the United States would relax its fears of a China threatening its allies and the sea lanes. The Chinese leadership might likewise eventually view the United States as less threatening.

Chinese military modernization could then focus less on countering U.S. military capabilities and more on homeland defense. Eventually, China might contribute to global public goods such as sea lane security. China would likely still want military power, but the United States would find the new capabilities of a liberalized China less threatening. In a truly benign scenario, China would build military capabilities that contribute to global security rather than threaten it.

Scenario 2: Somewhat Pessimistic

The second scenario involves only a modest change in trajectory from China's current path. In the first of two pessimistic scenarios, China's economic growth continues, but China remains authoritarian without meaningful change in the political and intellectual climate. Moreover, as China continues to develop, it shifts further toward a more aggressive external posture that presents economic and security challenges for the United States.

China continues along a relatively strong growth trajectory, with modest changes in its economic policies implemented to defuse growing imbalances in the financial system and in the composition of output. Any such changes will be taken cautiously and only as needed. China's leadership will not undertake the fundamental economic reforms as in the first scenario; as a result, growth will be somewhat slower than in the first scenario, though still fairly robust for years into the future as hundreds of millions of Chinese move from rural farms to urban industry. Growth would eventually slow as this internal migration ends, in part because the failure to proceed with further political and social liberalization would limit the growth of knowledge-intensive sectors. Without fundamental changes, the occurrence of an economic crisis cannot be ruled out, but this possibility is reserved for the third scenario.

This second scenario involves a continuation of elements of China's present growth strategy that are problematic for both China and the rest of the world. The tensions these policies engender will become increasingly difficult to address with ad hoc steps such as expensive bank rescues. Problematic policies would include:

- Mercantilist trade policy that exacerbates global tensions and reduces the gains from trade that would otherwise accrue to China and the United States. Political pressures could lead to a protectionist response in the United States and other countries in the event of China's failure to liberalize its domestic market in line with its commitments as part of the international trading system.

- Continued intervention in currency markets that eventually sparks a destructive trade war in which China, the United States, and other advanced economies that trade with China lose some of the current benefits of trade. Other countries intervene in currency markets as well, leading to a global race toward higher inflation.

- Lack of positive involvement in the global economic system, including the continued absence of a positive Chinese presence in trade negotiations such as the Doha Development Round and in other international economic forums such as the International Monetary Fund, and harmful involvement in the developing world by propping up unstable regimes such as in the Sudan, Venezuela, and Zimbabwe.

- China's failure to implement its World Trade Organization commitments, contributing to lower support for liberalization in the advanced economies. Ultimately, this continued failure to contribute to the global community fuels a backlash against trade and globalization.

- Heavy-handed political interference in the economy, resulting in the misallocation of resources and financial repression, in turn leading to continued excess saving in China. In the near term, this provides a subsidy to consumption in the rest of the world, but looking further ahead this gives rise to continued imbalances such as overspending in the United States and other advanced economies.

- Continued political and social repression, which would eventually affect sectors such as information technology, which inevitably would run up against barriers to growth as repression limits the dynamism of the private sector.

• Resource competition with the United States that drives up commodity prices and creates geopolitical tensions. Some of these tensions flow from Chinese business involvement in unstable areas and with problematic regimes.

Taken together, these developments pose serious concerns for the United States and the global economic system. In effect, they would undercut the gains to China and all countries from Chinese economic integration. This would be a turning back of the clocks to the early 1980s, before China's global presence in trade and investment provided economic benefits of faster growth, stronger productivity, and lower inflation for both China and its trading partners. The negative impact of weaker growth would be most pronounced in China, which has gained the most from global economic integration.

One key economic question in the second scenario relates to the reaction of the CCP when slowing economic growth leads to increased social disharmony within China. In this case, an attempt by the CCP to maintain political control may clash with the aspiration for further economic development.

Along with economic tensions come strategic problems. In the second scenario, China continues to grow but without developing the broader noneconomic connections to the rest of the world that would be expected with increased political and social liberalization. As in the first scenario, it would be natural to expect China to convert its economic growth to increased military and security expenditures, but these would be viewed as more threatening by the United States in the second scenario. Over time, China would assume an aggressive outward posture largely in line with the concerns of the national security approach to U.S.-China relations. Economic tensions would then lead to security ones, requiring a prolonged response from the United States that would demand a greater commitment of military and security resources.

A China able to muddle through economically with more illiberal internal policies could be the most difficult problem for the United States.

In this scenario, China is still growing and has mounting resources at its disposal but has chosen to reject the "liberal order," or at least limit its participation therein to the benefits it can accrue from limited trade. Of particular concern in this scenario is that problems inside China might be externalized. China, for example, might seek to force Taiwan into unification and claim additional spheres of influence for itself, such as the "first island chain." It would probably even more readily use high levels of violence to clamp down on unrest in places such as Tibet and Xinjiang. There are enough countries that would still satisfy China's need for commodities, but China would need a large ocean-going navy to protect its maritime traffic.

This scenario for China is the one that national security experts worry about because it implies that security competition intensifies and leads to a series of negative impacts throughout Asia.

Scenario 3: Very Pessimistic

In the most worrisome scenario, China's growth falters, and the Chinese leadership does not act in a timely or appropriate way to stave off the ensuing economic crisis. This crisis poses a political challenge to the Chinese leadership and the CCP, leading to an internal crackdown and an increasingly aggressive external posture as the leadership embarks on foreign "adventurism" to distract from its domestic failings.

Economic problems could arise in China through a sharp and sudden event resulting from financial imbalances and China's dependence on export-led growth, from inflationary pressures caused by the continued exchange rate peg, or from slow-building demographic pressures such as the aging of the population and the unbalanced numbers of men and women. These latter developments are likely to lead to wrenching changes in Chinese society over the coming decades, as the culmination of the one child policy leads to a collapse of extended networks of cousins and thus the breakdown of the Chinese family structure and the family-oriented social safety net. The surplus of men leads to societal pressures from millions of men who cannot marry; in response, the regime whips up antiforeign nationalism as a replacement for the social glue lost with the demise of the traditional Chinese family. A failure of the party leader-ship to adapt to such societal pressures could turn a slow demographic shift into an acute crisis.

On the economic side, a multidimensional crisis could start with slower export growth, perhaps as a result of slower growth in the rest of the world or a political-economy backlash against China caused by trade barriers imposed by the United States. At the same time, an external shock such as massively higher oil prices would lead to a slowdown in growth and a spike in inflation. This would combine with preexisting inflationary pressures from overly loose monetary policy to give a burst of inflation, which is the traditional harbinger of Chinese regime collapse (inflation played a key role in spurring unrest that culminated in regime changes in both 1911 and 1949).

In a political response but economic delusion, the leadership might then impose price and wage controls to stem inflation (ironically follow-ing in the misguided footsteps of President Richard Nixon). This would, in turn, lead to a drop in output as firms and farmers hold back on sell-ing their output at unprofitable prices. Financial problems would worsen the economic crisis as falling demand sours loan books at Chinese banks. A generalized financial panic could result from doubts over the willing-ness of the authorities to bail out banks, leading to a clamor as Chinese families jostle to pull their deposits. If the leadership hesitates to use its reserves to bail out banks, such a bank run could lead to a collapse of the Chinese financial system and have grave spillovers for the broader economy. Investment would freeze up, job creation and growth would slow, unemployment would rise sharply, and the ongoing migration from rural to urban would be disrupted.

There are many such potential scenarios in which economic growth reverses. Key elements could play out as a sharp and rapid crisis or as a longer souring of the Chinese growth model:

- Growth retreats sharply as the labor force shrinks in the after-math of the one child policy, while the legacy of poor lending leaves an industrial sector with inefficient factories and firms that cannot survive a stronger currency or trade disputes that close off foreign markets.

- Slower growth sparks a financial crisis as banks collapse from bad loans, and this sparks panicked withdrawals by depositors and a sudden suspension of investment. A run on the banking sector might be entirely reasonable given weak controls on lending, bubblelike prices of real estate, and a possible hesitation by the government to bail out faltering banks.

- Consumer and business spending collapses as Chinese families and businesses hoard resources.

- The Chinese government panics and responds by clamping down on private firms, further slowing growth.

- Foreign governments respond in kind to confiscation of foreign holdings and restrictions on international capital flows, and China loses access to key export markets. Prices would rise for U.S. and European consumers as their products are now sourced from high-cost suppliers in Latin America and Eastern Europe.

Such a dire scenario would threaten the stability of the regime by upending the implicit bargain under which the CCP rules in exchange for ensuring continued prosperity. These social pressures would have acute security implications, possibly including sparking active conflicts or grinding global tensions. This could arise, for example, if Chinese political leaders use external adventures to rally domestic support. In a context of unstable global relations, it could prove difficult to restart economic cooperation. A more aggressive China would find itself increasingly distrusted by other countries and excluded from the global economic system. This, in turn, would affect Chinese growth and further exacerbate external tensions.

In the third scenario, policy failures in China have global implications, leading to a worldwide economic downturn and sparking political and possibly military conflicts. This does not seem like a likely scenario, but it is based on a sequence of Chinese policy mistakes that are entirely possible and begin with a continuation of China's current misguided exchange rate peg.

A China under this kind of stress could go in three directions internally and externally. A strongman could emerge, most likely from the military, and then vast resources would be spent simply to hold the country together. In the fashion of Vladimir Putin, this leader could force his way onto the international stage through a more bellicose stance, perhaps even invading a neighbor (along the lines of the Russian invasion of Georgia) to signal that China will not be pushed around even as its economy slows. A more militaristic Chinese leadership could spend more money on defense, both to assert China's strategic presence and to stimulate the economy (though ultimately this would not be a path to sustainable growth). The Chinese leadership could use the surplus of males as a kind of praetorian guard or stronger internal security service that dials back the limited cultural or economic pluralism enjoyed today as the Iranian leadership employed its Revolutionary Guards (or as the Chinese leadership used the Red Guards in the 1960s). China, though decaying internally, would demand, and likely receive, a continued seat at international tables and try to ensure, through brute force or threats of force, the continued importation of vital commodities.

Another possibility under these conditions of economic downturn is a "soft" breakup of China, not necessarily in the manner of the Warlord Period, but more of a stagnant China trying to hold itself together. In this scenario, China would be marked more by armed gangs tied to local governments and to local and provincial party leaders. The world would see a struggle for scarce resources in China, such as water, as well as a struggle for control over ports to collect duties and tariffs. Central control of the military would be a question mark, and the United States would be left guessing who controls Chinese weapons of mass destruction.

Alternatively, and ironically, such an extreme case of economic disjuncture could in the end spark positive change. As Minxin Pei has written, China is in something of a "trap" in that any moves toward reform risk bringing down the party-state.[6] This seemingly very negative scenario could shock China into reform after a period of time. The key question would be whether there are enough reformers and liberals inside China—inside the party, inside business, and inside civil society—who could grab the reins of state before China reaches the precipice of economic and social disaster. If so, these groups could make a strong political case that the CCP has led China to utter disaster, and the only hope is a move toward the reforms envisioned in the first scenario. This is not impossible, given the kind of revolutionary changes that have occurred in Chinese history. It is worth remembering, however, that it took decades of internal distention and external attack for the Communists under Mao to enact the chairman's centralizing vision. A seeming collapse of China could break it out of its muddling-through policies, but the key question is whether the leaders exist, including within the PLA, who could take advantage of such a shock.

Conclusion

The key economic danger in the latter two scenarios is that China and the United States drift apart in a way that reduces the value of the bilateral economic relationship. If the United States were to impose ruinous trade sanctions, for example, this could lead China to focus on domestic growth, which might be good in itself, while closing itself off to foreign exports, which would be bad for China and other nations. Similarly, if China were to attempt to shut the United States out of a new Asian economic arrangement, this could lead to a sharp retrenchment of trade and global capital flows.

The key questions for U.S. policy revolve around how best to achieve the first scenario and avoid the third scenario. Much of the change must take place within China, including reforms of monetary and currency policy, removal of trade barriers, and opening the nation to free flows of capital, ideas, and political debates. On the economic side, one key U.S. contribution would be to increase U.S. national saving to reduce our dependence on foreign capital and thus to narrow our trade deficit. This would both provide a market-based impetus to move China away from export-led growth and also help avoid populist responses in both countries that could spur serious problems such as a trade war.

It is less clear how to shape China's path when there appears to be every economic incentive for China to move toward the cooperative path of the first scenario. The United States must also take into account that economic policymaking in China is mixed together with security policymaking and that policy decisions taken might not reflect a full understanding of any negative impacts on other nations. Chinese actions such as on energy policy are irresponsible, but this could reflect a lack of understanding rather than ill intent.

Even so, it would be prudent for the United States to recognize the clear possibilities of the second and third scenarios and thus prepare for continued political and strategic tensions. How the United States should prepare to deal with China in the coming decades is the topic of the next and final chapter.

Notes

1. Tarhan Feyzioglu explains that the Chinese banking system remains inefficient despite its profitability, with deposits tied up at large banks that do not provide effective financial intermediation across the economy. Low deposit rates and limited options for savers mean that the financial system does not provide Chinese families with efficient ways in which to safeguard their wealth and save for the future. See his "Does Good Financial Performance Mean Good Financial Intermediation in China?" (Working Paper WP/09/170, International Monetary Fund, 1999).

2. Guo and N'Diaye, "China's Export-Oriented Growth," 2009.

3. See Seymour M. Lipset, *Political Man: The Social Bases of Politics* (New York: Doubleday & Co., 1960); and Henry S. Rowen, "The Tide Underneath the 'Third Wave,'" *Journal of Democracy* 6, no. 1 (1995): 52–64.

4. Francis Fukuyama, *Trust: The Social Virtues and the Creation of Prosperity* (New York: Free Press, 1996).

5. Alexis de Tocqueville, "Of the Use Which the Americans Make of Public Associations in Civil Life," *Democracy in America*, part 2, chap. 5, trans. Harvey C. Mansfield and Delba Winthrop (Chicago: University of Chicago Press, 2002), 187–217.

6. Minxin Pei, *China's Trapped Transition: The Limits of Developmental Autocracy* (Cambridge, MA: Harvard University Press, 2008).

5

Dealing with China in the Future

Dan Blumenthal and Phillip Swagel

China is both an economic partner and a strategic rival. As China continues to develop, its relationship with the United States will be marked by the contradictory forces of parallel economic cooperation and security rivalry. China's military modernization, its treatment of its citizens, its intentions with respect to Taiwan, and its troublesome external behavior toward U.S. allies and international pariahs all reveal a Beijing that looks to upend the liberal international order to America's detriment. This is the irresponsible side of China. On the other hand, China benefits enormously from its economic engagement with the United States and its participation in the global trade and financial systems. Beijing's economic incentives for ensuring stability are significant. Still, the reality is that economic incentives alone do not drive Chinese policy; nationalism, regime insecurity, and China's unique worldview likewise play an important role in Beijing's decision-making process.

In some ways, this duality mirrors China's contradictory view of itself. China is both strong and weak. China's people and government have understandable pride in the material accomplishments achieved over the past three decades and hold the view that the rest of the world should see China as a strong country ready to take its place in the global system. At the same time, however, China reverts to an image of a weak and still-developing country when it seeks to avoid the responsibilities that come with being a global economic powerhouse and an international economic system stakeholder that should ease global tensions. China often mentions its past disadvantages relative to the West as an excuse for shirking international responsibility. Indeed, as noted in earlier chapters, China views Western insistence on its adherence to international norms and its shouldering the burden of global issues as attempts to control its internal political dynamics and unique path of development.

The duality of strong and weak comes across in policy terms, with China seeking at times to be seen as master of its policies and at others as helplessly subject to external shocks. Chinese authorities sometimes protest that they are buffeted by outside events and cannot take the appropriate actions sought by counterparts in the United States. In the face of the financial crisis in 2008, for example, China reverted to a currency peg against the dollar. It wanted to maintain its own stability even though this action removed what would have been useful flexibility for global adjustment, since a stronger renminbi and weaker dollar would have usefully boosted growth in the United States through increased exports. After the worst impact of the crisis passed, however, China was very much in control in deciding when it would resume a currency appreciation.

The Task for U.S. Policy

As the world's two largest economies, the United States and China are bound together through a string of economic and financial ties—sometimes awkwardly and with irritations, but on the whole for the common good of the two countries. This need not be the case in the future. The challenge for U.S. policy is to ensure that the future relationship with China is benign and productive rather than antagonistic.

In the face of these divergent aspects of Chinese self-image and policy-making, the United States would do well to deal with China on separate economic and security tracks in the bilateral relationship. The United States should continue to engage China in the economic relationship, even while holding China to high standards in areas such as protection of intellectual property rights and adherence to international treaty obligations. But there should be no illusion that an improved relationship on the economic side will, by itself, lead Chinese policymakers away from global adventurism in areas such as Iran and Sudan. Instead, the United States must develop tools that will present China with choices and consequences for provocative behavior. Continued Chinese investments in Iranian energy fields, for example, should lead to aggressive financial pressures on the Chinese companies involved, and on their bankers, suppliers, and shippers. This will sometimes be uncomfortable for U.S. firms dealing with Chinese businesses, but the economic relationship is valuable in both directions, and thus China has substantial incentives to avoid allowing national security frictions to spill over into the economic relationship.

On key global security issues, there is little hope that China will play a constructive role in areas such as containing the Iranian and North Korean nuclear threats. The PRC has demonstrated repeatedly that it is a free rider in such situations: it hopes to expand commercial relations with these renegade states even while expecting the United States to take the costly and difficult actions to contain these two regimes.

Given the likelihood of continued strong Chinese growth for the next several years, the American strategic response to China will inevitably involve creating forces and building alliances that deter China from undertaking aggressive actions. This policy approach is different from Cold War containment as outlined by George Kennan in his Long Telegram about U.S. policy toward the Soviets. The policy aim in that instance was to defeat the Soviet Union and roll back its empire. There was no thought given to changing the Soviet Union or bringing it into the liberal system. Instead, the objective was to break its model and only then to consider the future place of post-Soviet Russia in the international system.

China, in contrast to the Soviet Union, has taken considerable steps to fit into the global economy. There is now a strong existing international system that is based on rules and norms of sovereign behavior. This is a system designed for states that play by the rules, live up to their obligations, and settle disputes peacefully. Democracy and respect for the intellectual freedom of one's own people are parts of the international system. On this count, obviously, Chinese participation is found wanting.

The objective now should be to bring China fully into that system so that it plays a constructive role. Alongside this objective, the United States must work to strengthen the international system such that it is robust enough to withstand challenges such as attempts to use commercial diplomacy to split off U.S. allies. The United States and its Asian allies must maintain sufficient military capabilities to deter China from destabilizing Asia. Moreover, the United States must ensure that there is broad international agreement on the rules that define the Western-led international system, including economic rules, access to energy and commodity resources, peaceful conduct, and democratic practice. Even in the wake of the global financial crisis and in the face of ongoing economic challenges in Europe and the United States, the Western-led system remains strong. Over time, however, the system will atrophy if not properly defended.

U.S. economic and security policies, if tailored properly, should convey a clear message to Beijing: China is welcome to integrate itself more fully into the global economic and security system from which it benefits, but there are consequences for destabilizing the system, whether by intent or by neglect. These consequences, imposed by the United States and its Asian partners, would be modest at first and designed to make China lose face. Such actions could include mild diplomatic sanctions or disinvitations from regional or global summits. But more serious steps would be taken should Chinese behavior become more actively provocative. Other countries in Asia are preparing to act if needed. India, Australia, and Singapore, for example, are arming in response to China. Others, such as Vietnam, are realizing the need to do so.

Separating the economic and security tracks means that the United States should seek to maximize the benefits of the bilateral economic relationship. But U.S. policymakers should not be afraid to use economic and financial tools as levers to affect Chinese behavior. Regarding the North Korea problem, for example, the United States took serious actions in 2005 by cutting off the financial system of Macau in response to the trail of laundered North Korean money, freezing $24 million in North Korean assets in the Bank of Macau.[1] This step changed Chinese behavior: Beijing began taking seriously North Korean counterfeiting activities that would have posed a risk to the dollar-based international financial regime. If China is doing something wrong, Washington should not hesitate to adopt an appropriate policy response, keeping in mind that China needs the economic relationship just as much as the United States does.

Above all, the United States must reengage Asian governments and take the reins of economic and security leadership in the region. With the ultimate goal of a pan-Asian free trade agreement (FTA), Washington should continue to build upon its recently ratified FTAs with nations such as South Korea and Singapore by negotiating them with other nations and by continuing to lead the multilateral Trans-Pacific Partnership negotiations. The United States should also revitalize its economic relationship with Japan and assist Tokyo in implementing policies that will foster renewed growth; Washington should support a Japanese monetary policy that reverses the strong yen, even though this will have consequences for U.S. exports. The overriding need is for Japan to grow again.

U.S. leadership in Asia would not exclude Chinese participation in regional affairs but rather provide a strong framework within which to include China while ensuring that the United States is also included in all important regional arrangements.

In providing security leadership in Asia, the challenge for the United States is to build meaningful hedges against Chinese military adventurism. Washington must ensure it has the military forces needed to reassure allies and partners in Asia, to deter Chinese aggression, and to defeat PLA forces if need be. Given the nature of the theater, maritime and air forces in particular should be properly resourced.

The U.S. Navy must be able to defend against Chinese antiship ballistic and cruise missiles and to project power into Asian littorals. Though aircraft carriers have not lost their utility, smaller, fast, stealthy vessels can perform a variety of missions, including antisubmarine and antisurface warfare. There is, in particular, a need for large numbers of submarines, the only vessels that can operate at low risk in the face of Chinese antiaccess capabilities.

New air power capabilities are needed as well. The Department of Defense should continue its commitment to the F-35 Joint Strike Fighter for the Navy, Air Force, and Marine Corps. With the exception of the F-22, of which there are few, the fighters currently fielded by U.S. forces are no longer in a class of their own. To maintain the ability to achieve air dominance where and when the United States wishes, large numbers of modern stealth fighters are necessary. The short-take-off-and-vertical-landing (STOVL) variant of the F-35 airframe is especially relevant to the Asia-Pacific theater. Because its STOVL capability would mitigate the effectiveness of missile attacks on runways, it is important that this platform be maintained.

The missile threat, which is in part driving the above requirements, also necessitates renewed investment in missile defense. Directed energy technology is promising, and research and development should be funded accordingly. Put simply, on the whole the United States should invest in the capabilities it needs to ensure its continued military predominance in Asia.

To hedge against Chinese belligerence, the United States must also engage with its regional partners, such as Australia, Japan, India, the Philippines, Vietnam, Singapore, and South Korea, to determine what Chinese activities would merit consequences. In particular, Washington should work to knit a tighter web of regional allies that may assist each other's self-defense capabilities. This requires revising U.S. export control practices to make it easier to sell defense equipment to security partners and requires that future weapons systems generally be designed with the potential for export in mind.

While some of America's friends in Asia still share historical animosities—South Korea and Japan, for example—Washington can facilitate cooperation, which in turn may help dispel lingering antagonisms. To facilitate broad-based cooperation among partners, the United States should work to establish a regional intelligence, surveillance, and reconnaissance network. Such a network would be based on U.S. technology and would pool partners' resources so that all U.S. friends would have a common operating picture of the Asia-Pacific.

The overall strategy is to convince China that the costs of aggression are unacceptably high, both by making individual states more able to defend themselves and by demonstrating to Beijing that aggression against one U.S. partner is seen as aggression against all.

The United States should also embark on a long-term project to boost Chinese civil society and thereby help bring about a democratic China. U.S. political and cultural leaders must find ways to engage Chinese actors outside of the CCP and stress consistently the need for independent institutions in China such as churches, a judiciary, and so on. No U.S. president should ever visit China again without demanding to visit religious groups and civic organizations. Neither should any president ever have his remarks censored by the Chinese government. There is no need to be bashful about our long-term interest in a free and democratic China.

If the worst comes about, the United States must be ready to react to negative developments such as the second and third scenarios. These reactions would involve military containment and actions that impose costs on China. The Chinese have many fears that can be exploited: separatism, encirclement, internal subversion, and domestic unrest. Washington should develop an escalation ladder to respond to provocative Chinese actions; U.S. policy options would range from warming ties with Taipei to engaging activists in Tibet and Xinjiang. The United States could also take a more active role in disseminating information into China on elite corruption. If the Chinese appear willing to start a conflict over their manifold territorial claims, the United States should work with its allies to demonstrate that all are prepared to engage in a protracted conflict, at any temperature, that would result in limiting China's economic and strategic potential.

Washington has no quarrel with the Chinese people, who have accomplished so much over the past decades. But actions of the CCP's elite are often worrisome. The United States has never before faced such a dynamic society with which it is both deeply engaged in economic and financial matters and enmeshed in a competition in the security sphere. Meeting the challenge will require a deftness that will call upon the best of American statecraft.

Note

1. For an overview, see Emma Chanlett-Avery, "North Korea: U.S. Relations, Nuclear Program, and Internal Situation," Congressional Research Service, January 17, 2012.

About the Authors

Dan Blumenthal is the Director of Asian Studies at the American Enterprise Institute, which he joined in November 2004. He has served on the U.S.-China Economic and Security Commission since 2005, including as a vice chair in 2007. He has also served as a member of the Academic Advisory Board for the Congressional U.S.-China Working Group. Previously, he was senior director for China, Taiwan, and Mongolia in the Office of the Secretary of Defense for international security affairs during the first George W. Bush administration. He is widely published, with written articles and op-eds appearing in the *Washington Post,* the *Wall Street Journal,* the *Weekly Standard,* the *National Review, Foreign Policy*, and other publications. He has also contributed chapters to numerous edited volumes. This is his first book.

Phillip Swagel is a professor of international economics at the University of Maryland's School of Public Policy and a visiting scholar at the American Enterprise Institute. He was previously assistant secretary for economic policy at the Treasury Department from 2006 to 2009, where he was responsible for analysis on a wide range of economic issues, including policies relating to the financial crisis and the Troubled Asset Relief Program. He has also served as chief of staff and senior economist at the White House Council of Economic Advisers and as an economist at the Federal Reserve Board and the International Monetary Fund. He has previously taught at Northwestern University, the University of Chicago's Booth School of Business, and Georgetown University. Swagel works on both domestic and international economic issues at the American Enterprise Institute. His research topics include financial markets reform, international trade policy, and the role of China in the global economy.